The Persian Gulf

Westview Special Studies on the Middle East

The Persian Gulf:
An Introduction to Its Peoples, Politics, and Economics
David E. Long

Since the energy crisis of 1973, the political, economic, and strategic importance of the Persian Gulf to U.S. interests has become readily apparent. Yet little has been written on the area or on policy considerations toward it. This book, in its second, updated edition, fills a considerable part of the gap in the literature. The first chapter describes the geographical and climatic features of the region, its peoples, and their cultures. Other chapters analyze the dynamics of each of the littoral states; regional gulf politics, centering on the clash of radicalism and conservatism on the one hand and that of Persian and Arab nationalism on the other; the role of the gulf in international politics; gulf oil; and the economics of the region. The final chapter deals with U.S. interests in the area, recent strategic and economic moves, the development of a U.S. gulf policy over the last nine years, and an assessment of that policy in terms of future national needs.

David E. Long, a research analyst with the Department of State, was previously executive director of the Center for Contemporary Arab Studies, Georgetown University. Dr. Long holds an M.A. degree from the Fletcher School of Law and Diplomacy and a Ph.D. from George Washington University. He is currently working with Dr. Bernard Reich on a text on the government and politics of the Middle East.

Revised Edition

The Persian Gulf

An Introduction to Its Peoples, Politics, and Economics

David E. Long

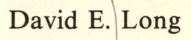

Westview Press • Boulder, Colorado

Westview Special Studies on the Middle East

Copyright © 1976, 1978 by Westview Press, Inc.

Published in 1978 in the United States of America by

Westview Press, Inc.
5500 Central Avenue
Boulder, Colorado 80301
Frederick A. Praeger, Publisher and Editorial Director

Library of Congress Cataloging in Publication Data
Long, David E
    The Persian Gulf.
    (Westview special studies on the Middle East)
    Bibliography: p.
    1. Persian Gulf region. 2. Persian Gulf region—Politics and government. I. Title.
DS326.L654   1978   953'.6   77-14059
ISBN 0-89158-826-4

Printed and bound in the United States of America

To Barbara, Gordon, Geoffrey, and Andrew

Contents

Preface to the Revised Edition

Looking back over the year and a half since this book was completed, I find it very difficult to evaluate the lasting significance of the many changes that have taken place. One could make a convincing case that the gulf area has totally changed, but an equally convincing case could be made that all is the same.

There have been no major governmental changes in the region, although several of the gulf rulers are in ill health and changes could occur in the next few years. On the international scene, the Arab-Israeli problem has become a far greater factor in gulf politics than it had been. Economically, the petrodollar has continued to grow in importance. At the same time, the almost hysterical predictions of economic chaos that one heard in 1974 and 1975, resulting from the gulf oil producers' accumulation of foreign reserves, have given way to a more realistic appreciation of petro-economics. Thus, looking at the gulf area in the summer of 1977, I would have to say that, on balance, it continues to enjoy a level of tranquility quite singular for the Middle East.

I should like to thank Deborah Miller, David Vance, and Peter Johnson for their help in revising and updating the text.

Burke, Virginia
August 1977

Acknowledgments

Anyone who attempts a broad survey study is beholden to more people than he can mention. This survey is no exception. That it was done at all was due to the Council on Foreign Relations which provided me an International Affairs Fellowship for 1974-1975. I should especially like to thank Alton Frye and John Campbell of the council for their support and encouragement. Thanks are also extended to David Abshire and the Georgetown University Center for Strategic and International Studies for so graciously providing me with a place to write and conduct research and for the excellent administrative support during my fellowship year, and to Jon Vondracek of the center for his unflagging support and encouragement. I am indebted to Richard Erb, another International Affairs Fellow and a traveling companion during our research trip to the gulf, for his excellent company and enlightenment on some of the mysteries of "petroeconomics." He also provided the economic data in the Appendix. The support and kindness of my Foreign Service colleagues all along the way—the Jack Pattersons in Tehran, who put us up for a night when we had nowhere else to go; the American Embassy staffs in Kuwait, Bahrain, Qatar, UAE, Oman (where Bob Headly also put me up and David Zweifel got me to Dhufar and Nizwa), Saudi Arabia, Lebanon, and London —all were invaluable. The embassy staffs and government officials of each of the gulf states we visited were more than generous with their time and assistance; I cannot thank them enough. I also wish to thank those of the Arabian Mission of the Reformed Church in America for their kindness and help, particularly Dr. Donald Bosch in Muscat. To Debbie Dawson, Mona Jallad, John Wetter, and particularly Blythe Jones—who suffered through deciphering most of the first draft—I gratefully acknowledge my appreciation for the willingness and cheerfulness with which they prepared the manuscript, and to Michael Burrell and Thomas Ricks, who read it in its entirety and offered valuable suggestions, I also say thank you. Finally, I should like to give my humble thanks to my family for bearing with me during the months of research, travel, and writing that went into the book.

Georgetown University
February 1976

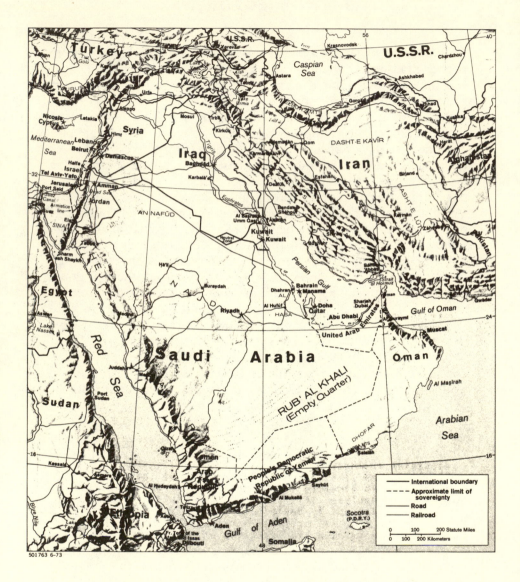

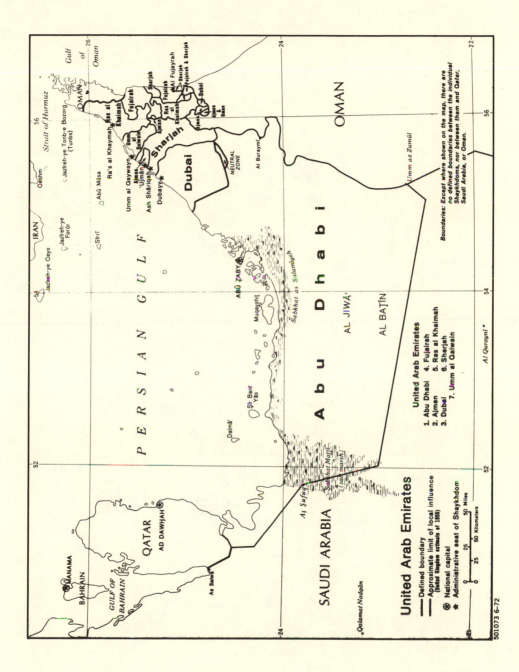

Boundaries: Except where shown on the map, there are no defined boundaries between the individual Shaykhdoms, nor between them and Qatar, Saudi Arabia, or Oman.

OMAN

Gulf of Oman

Strait of Hormuz

Qeshm

Jazīreh-ye Tonb-e Bozorg (Tunbs)

Abū Mūsā

Jazīreh-ye Forūr

Sirrī

IRAN

Jazīreh-ye Qeys

Sharjah

Dubai

Ra's al Khaymah

Umm al Qaywayn
Ajman
'Ujmān
Ash Shāriqah
Dubayy

Al Buraymī

NEUTRAL ZONE

Umm az Zumūl

P E R S I A N   G U L F

Sabkhat as Salamīyah

A b u   D h a b i

ABŪ ZABY

Muqayshiţ

Sīr Banī Yās

Dalmā'

AL JIWĀ'

AL BAŢIN

OMAN

As Sufūq

Sabkhat Maţţi
(salt marsh)

Al Quraymī*

SAUDI ARABIA

Qalamat Nadqān

QATAR

AD DAWHAH

BAHRAIN

MANAMA

GULF OF BAHRAIN

As Salwá

United Arab Emirates

1. Abu Dhabi
2. Ajman
3. Dubai
4. Fujairah
5. Ras al Khaimah
6. Sharjah
7. Umm al Qaiwain

United Arab Emirates

—— Defined boundary

—— Approximate limit of local influence
(based Kingdom estimate of 1955)

⊛ National capital

★ Administrative seat of Shaykhdom

0   25   50 Miles

0   25   50 Kilometers

501073 6-72

1
The Land and People

Geography, in the words of Carlton Coon, "is the prince of disciplines, combining the fruits of geology, meteorology, anthropology, sociology, economics, and dozens of other specialties."[1] Nowhere else in the world is there a better example of the impact of geography on society, economics, and politics than the Persian Gulf. Start with geology. The gulf is situated in a sedimentary basin which holds roughly two-thirds of the world's proven reserves of oil. Without that fact, the gulf would elicit little interest for any but the peoples who inhabit its shores. But because of its oil, in an energy-deficient world, it has become an area of universal importance. Understanding the peoples of the gulf has taken on an urgency never known before. And to understand them, because their societies have been molded by the lands they live in, it is necessary to start with their geography.

Stretching from Turkey to Oman, the Persian Gulf juts like a broken finger northwestward from the Gulf of Oman to the marshes of the Shatt al-Arab River. Roughly 90,000 square miles in area, it is 600 miles long and 230 miles across at its widest point. With no discernable channel or thalweg, it is shaped like a flat, shallow basin never exceeding 300 feet in depth.

The shores of the gulf are generally inhospitable, swampy in the north and desert elsewhere, occasionally broken by salt flats called *sabkhas*. The coastal population is primarily located in scattered oasis towns. Except where oil revenues have financed large-scale desalination, the lack of sweet water is the primary curb on the population growth.

Inland to the east, the Zagros Mountains separate the gulf from the high, arid plateau of central Iran. In the north, the Zagros meet the Elburz range of northern Iran, with its Mount Demavend, towering to 18,934 feet. The northern slopes of the Elburz drop off sharply to the Caspian Sea, some 85 feet below sea level, forming a lush, semitropical area rich in agriculture. To the northwest of the Gulf, beyond the marshes, lies the Mesopotamian valley of Iraq, through which flow the Tigris and Euphrates rivers until they join to form the Shatt al-Arab. Bounded on the east by the Zagros Mountains, on the west by the Syrian desert, and stretching toward the Taurus Mountains of Turkey, this valley was one of the breadbaskets of the ancient Middle East. With massive inputs of oil revenue in Iraq and a world shortage of food to spur investment, it may become so again.

The western shore of the gulf, which forms the eastern side of the Arabian Peninsula, is shaped like a giant fishhook. The Musandam Peninsula forms the tip, and the Qatar Peninsula extends northward to form the barb. Between the northern tip of Qatar and the Saudi Arabian mainland lies the Bahrain archipelago. The northern end of Bahrain is an oasis fed by underground water from the mainland, an extension of the Qatif Oasis on the Saudi side. With the extensive use of water for oil and other industries on both sides, the water table is dropping; if nothing is done, in a few years Bahrain could face a severe water shortage curtailing its agriculture.

Inland from the Saudi coast adjacent to Qatar is the great al-Hasa (or Ahsa) oasis and its principal town, Hufuf, with its crinolated mud-brick walls and forts. To the west is Najd, the Arabian heartland, dotted with oasis towns and Riyadh, the Saudi capital. Najd, bisected by an escarpment, Jabal Tuwayq, which extends 600 miles in a shallow arc from north to south, is bounded by two great pink-sand deserts, the Great Nafud in the north and the Rub' al-Khali or Empty Quarter in the south. The deserts are connected by a narrow strip, the Dahna, which extends north to south between Najd and al-Hasa. West of Najd lie the Hijaz Mountains, the

Islamic holy places of Mecca and al-Medinah, and the Red Sea. The mountains form an escarpment inland from the Red Sea coastal plain. They reach an elevation of over 10,000 feet in Asir, and in the Yemen, south of Saudi Arabia, exceed 12,000 feet.

The area south of the gulf and east of the Rub' al-Khali is historical Oman, now divided into the United Arab Emirates (UAE) in the north and the Sultanate of Oman in the south. As if to complement the heights of Yemen, Oman also boasts a mountain range, the Hajar, divided into eastern and western ranges and crowned by Jabal Akhdar (Green Mountain), which exceeds 10,000 feet. These mountains curve, as Coon describes them, "like a stray member of the Zagros pack trying to rejoin its fellows."[2] East of the mountains on the Gulf of Oman is the Batinah Coast. Westward lies "Inner Oman," long isolated from the rest of the country. To the south along the Arabian Sea coast are the Qara Mountains of Dhufar, and to the west of Dhufar lie the Hadhramaut, Aden, and again the Yemeni highlands.

The climate of the gulf is harsh and, except in the mountains, generally arid. Summer temperatures (May to October) average over 115 degrees Fahrenheit in many areas and can reach 130. During a week-long sandstorm in Riyadh one summer, I saw a thermometer read 145 degrees. Some relief is found at night, when the temperature may drop as much as 50 degrees.

Contrary to the ideas of many Westerners, however, the climate is not always hot and dry. Along the coast, although the average annual rainfall is only three to six inches, the summer months are very muggy; the humidity sometimes stays at 100 percent for days. During such periods, temperatures seldom climb above 110 degrees, but as the moisture holds the heat, neither do they fall much below 100 degrees at night.

In the winter months, the climate is quite balmy. Daytime temperatures reach into the 90s, but with low humidity it is very pleasant. Many residents of the area find it too cold in the winter to swim because, even with the temperature at 95 degrees, the water on the body evaporates so fast in the dry air as to make one shiver. At night, winter temperatures drop very rapidly, and it is not uncommon for them to dip below freezing.

The climate in the mountains is, of course, much colder, and in most cases there is more rainfall. Rainfall, or the lack of it, has been the greatest single factor in molding the societies of the gulf. Precipitation is brought by two prevailing wind systems: the winter westerlies from the Atlantic and the summer monsoons from the Indian Ocean. The westerlies, having lost most of their moisture in Europe and the mountains of North Africa and the Levant, are very fickle by the time they reach the Zagros and Hajar mountains. Areas where twenty or more inches of rain have fallen annually for decades may go without any for one, two or five years. At other times, torrential downpours may cause flash floods, wiping out farms and villages. The lesson of undependable rains was well known in ancient times, when great storehouses were filled with food for the inevitable "years of want." In modern times, their lesson is reflected in the culverts and bridges which desert road builders construct over dry wadis (valleys and streambeds). Several years ago, a road engineer in Saudi Arabia who did not allow properly for the rains looked on helplessly as miles and miles of road were either washed out or blocked by the flow of waters from desert downpours. He suffered the ultimate indignity when even his own construction camp was flooded out.

The monsoons have all the dependability that the westerlies do not. Half the year they blow in a northerly direction, bringing moisture from the Indian Ocean. The other half of the year their direction is reversed. Unfortunately, the monsoons are of little benefit to the gulf region. While dumping vast amounts of rain on the Indian subcontinent to the east and the Ethiopian highlands to the west, in between they provide rain only on the Qara Mountains of Dhufar and the Yemeni and Asiri highlands. In another way, however, they have probably had as decisive an influence on the patterns of life in the gulf as any other factor. As we have seen, the area is one of mountains, desert, and an inhospitable climate. Since history began, this terrain has impeded travel and, particularly in the mountains, harbored brigands and rebel groups. The waters of the gulf, on the other hand, provided an avenue of communication and trade as Arab dhows sailed southward with the monsoons, out into the Indian Ocean to the Indian subcontinent and East African coast. When the winds changed six months later, the dhows sailed home again. Until just recently, therefore, the major external focus of the gulf was south and east, not north or west.

The peoples who inhabit this fabulously wealthy but inhospitable land share elements of a common heritage. Perhaps the single most important such element is Islam. The hold of Islam on the peoples of the Middle East cannot be overestimated, even on those who no longer are practicing believers. More than a religion, it is an entire way of life. In Islam, there is no distinction between sacred and secular. All things are the will of God. This has imbued Islamic society with a highly developed sense of fatalism. Not to be confused with defeatism, fanaticism, or passivism, this fatalism rather instills in the Muslim a sense of the inevitability of things.

The peoples of the gulf, as elsewhere in the Middle East, are oriented more closely to their extended families and tribal groupings than to any other sociopolitical structure such as province, state, region, or in the case of the Arabs, the Arab world. Above all, obligations to one's kin, regardless of political allegiances, come first.

When Americans hear the word *tribe* used in conjunction with the Middle East, it generally evokes the image of a country of desert nomads plodding along with their camels and their wives from oasis to oasis. To be sure, each of the gulf littoral states has nomadic tribesmen within its borders. But the nomadic tribe is not the decisive social force in the area. It is in the sedentary population centers that the culture of the area has its roots. It is true, however, that even the sedentary people claim a tribal lineage back to some dim, if not entirely mythological, ancestor. And for almost all, marriage and family relations reflect the dominant influence of family ties. Among the many Arabs, for instance, marriage within the extended family is more highly regarded than marriage without, and marriage to a first cousin is most highly regarded of all. Moreover, even in cities it is not uncommon for extended families to live in compounds—as many as a dozen nuclear families of uncles, cousins, and brothers all clustered together.

Another common element among the peoples of the gulf is the increasing disruption of traditional social patterns through the process of modernization. Nearly every country in the area is making a major effort to stamp out illiteracy and upgrade the standard of living. A new class of cosmopolitan and sophisticated elites has emerged in the government, the military, and the private sector, and a new class of proletarian workers can be seen in the oil fields and major cities.

Accompanying modernization is the trend toward urbanization. Urban centers are not new to the gulf area. Most of the gulf shaykhdoms were city-states from the start, and Baghdad has always been the population center of Iraq. Iran, Saudi Arabia, and Oman each possess several old and proud cities. But the last quarter-century has seen a large-scale expansion. From 1945, Tehran has grown from a mud-brick city of 100,000 to a metropolis of 3.3 million—one of every ten Iranians—and is growing by about 200,000 people a year. Riyadh has also grown from a mud-brick desert town to a city of nearly a half-million, surpassing Mecca and Jidda in size. In Oman, emerging from a cocoon of medievalism with the accession of Sultan Qabus in 1970, the capital, Muscat, has expanded as far as the mountains surrounding it on the land side will allow, and its sister city Mutrah is now becoming the country's major urban center.

Modernization is proceeding within and among different countries at different paces. Even in Iran, where the shah's development plan, the White Revolution, has produced spectacular results in some areas, most of the population is still nonurban and illiterate, and several million are still nomadic tribesmen. At the opposite pole are the nonoil shaykhdoms of the UAE and parts of Oman where the modernization process has barely begun.

Education, travel, urbanization, and other aspects of modernization, largely made possible by oil money, may eventually break down the traditional social system. But the process will take longer than even the most ardent disciples of development may be willing to admit. As the old saying goes, it is far easier to get the boy out of the country than the country out of the boy.

Also common to the gulf peoples, and to Middle Easterners as a whole, is the tendency to be more person related than problem related, in contrast to the emphasis on problem solving so prevalent in the West. This is the result of a highly developed sense of family consciousness, the Islamic belief in the inevitability of life, and perhaps a host of other factors as well. In his business and personal interactions, for example, someone from the gulf, when answering a question, would probably give more attention to what he thinks the questioner wishes to hear than to the substance of the question. He will also be careful to prevent even his adversaries from losing face. Major policy decisions are often made on the basis of personal relationships and animosities. Therefore, to attribute to gulf economic and oil policies the same type of cost-benefit analysis that Western economists might apply, or to take at face value policy statements designed to put the best face on an unpalatable policy, can be very risky. Unlike many of their advisors, no gulf rulers have graduate degrees in business or economics from American or other universities. (The only gulf ruler with any university degree is Shaykh Sultan of Sharjah.) And it is the rulers, not their advisors, who make policy.

To the outsider, the similarities of the peoples of the gulf could overshadow differences which in fact may be highly significant. For example, though nearly all of the gulf peoples are Muslim, they are divided by the great Sunni-Shi'a schism. Nine of ten Iranians and a majority of Iraqis and Bahrainis are Shi'a, or heterodox, Muslims. Shi'a Islam is the official state religion of Iran. The Saudis, Kuwaitis, and the native populations of the lower gulf are mostly Sunni, or orthodox, Muslims. Most Omanis follow the Ibadi sect, which is neither Sunni nor Shi'a, but the only surviving descendent of an even earlier schism, the Kharijite movement. Religious differences in the gulf do not have the direct political implications that, for example, they do in Northern Ireland. But in the gulf, allegiance to a particular religious group is a major determinant of one's sense of identity. And a sense of identity is the basic building block upon which loyalty to the state is constructed.

The most visible difference among peoples of the gulf is in ethnic and national heritage. The eastern side of the gulf is Persian, and the western side is Arab. At the same time, upon closer scrutiny this distinction becomes blurred. One hears Farsi (Persian) as much as Arabic in the *suqs* ("markets") of Doha, the capital of Qatar; and Arabic is the native language of many Iranian citizens on Iran's gulf coast and northward into Khuzistan and Fars. Baluchi, Urdu, Turkic dialects, and many nongulf dialects of Arabic are also heard frequently, as are the languages of western oil men, businessmen, advisors, and government officials serving in the gulf. With the dhow trade well entrenched since ancient times, the gulf has always been a cosmopolitan place. Since the coming of the oil industry, it has become one of the most heterogeneous places on earth. Indeed, in oil shaykhdoms such as Kuwait and Abu Dhabi, the resident alien population actually outnumbers the native population.

In addition to these general characteristics and differences, the societies of each of the gulf states have their own separate identities and therefore their own political dynamics. The following are merely brief sketches of an extremely complex subject.

Iran

About half of the 33 million inhabitants of Iran speak Persian as their native language, and Persian is Iran's official language. The vast expansion of public education, in which Persian language, history, and culture are emphasized, has greatly accelerated the growing Persian cultural predominance in the country.

There are, however, a number of different tribal and ethnic areas which ring the Persian heartland. In the northwest are the Turkic-speaking Azeris, kinsmen of those living in neighboring Soviet Azerbaijan. (In 1946 the Soviets tried unsuccessfully to annex the Iranian Azeris by attempting to establish a so-called Azerbaijan Republic with Tabriz as the capital.) In northeast Iran are Turkoman tribesmen, also with blood ties over the Soviet border. In the central Zagros southwest of Isfahan are the Bakhtiari tribes, and west of them to the Iraqi border are the Lurs; both speak a dialect of Persian. In the southern Zagros are the Turkic-speaking Qashqa'is.

Three ethnic groups in Iran are of particular interest to the study of the gulf. Most of the peoples along the Iranian coast of the gulf and in Khuzistan east of the Shatt al-Arab speak Arabic although many are also bilingual in Persian. Called Hawalah Arabs, many are Sunni Muslims and have close ethnic and historical ties with the Arab side of the gulf. A whole segment of the Bahrainis, for example, are originally from this area and are called locally "Lingawis," after Lingeh, a town on the Iranian coast.

North of Khuzistan and the Lurs' tribal area are the Kurds. Also Sunni Muslims, their historical tribal area includes parts of Iraq and Turkey as well as Iran. (After World War II, the Soviets also tried unsuccessfully to promote a Kurdish "republic" in Iran.) It is the role of the Kurds in Iraqi-Iranian relations that has had an impact on recent Gulf politics. The shah's support for Iraqi Kurds in their demand for local autonomy has been a principal cause of the hostile state of relations between Iraq and Iran. Although this support has been withdrawn, causing the latest Kurdish uprising to subside, the potential for Iranian involvement in Iraqi-Kurdish affairs still remains.

The Baluchi tribes of southeastern Iran also figure prominently in gulf society and politics. Mostly Sunni Muslims, they are located on both sides of the Iranian-Pakistani border and north into Afghanistan and inhabit some of the most barren, desolate pieces of real estate in the world. For centuries, Baluchis have crossed the Gulf of Oman to settle on Oman's Batinah Coast. More recently they have been drawn to the gulf oil shaykhdoms by the relatively high wages for manual labor. It has also been the practice for Baluchis to be recruited in Pakistan by the British to serve in Oman's armed forces.

Three other ethnic groups should be mentioned. Though small in number, the Jewish community is comparatively well off in Iran. The tolerance with which they are treated is a reflection of Iranian acceptance, if not support, of world Jewish aspirations and the right of Israel to exist. There are also small communities of Armenian Christians and Zoroastrians. The latter still follow the pre-Islamic religion of Persia.

Iraq

Three-fourths of the population of Iraq is Arab, but that does not give the degree of homogeneity to the population that it might suggest. The largest minority ethnic group is the Kurds, roughly 15 percent of the population. For years the Kurds have agitated for autonomy under their leader, Mullah Mustafah Barzani. In March 1971 an agreement giving the Kurds various rights was reached between the Kurds and the Iraqi government, but by 1974 the accord had broken down, and Kurdish insurgency, aided by Iran, had risen again. In March 1975, after Iranian support was stopped, the Kurdish insurgency again collapsed, and Barzani sought exile outside Iraq.

Even among the Iraqi Arabs, there is little unity. Those living in the west are mostly nomadic, belonging to the great tribal confederations which extend from the deserts of Iraq, Syria, and Jordan, south into Saudi Arabia. In the marshes of southern Iraq, the "Marsh Arabs" live in small groups of huts kept above water by rushes which must constantly be replaced. They are seminomadic people who drive their water buffalo into the marshes in the winter and retreat with the high waters to the river banks in the summer.

Most of the Arabs, indeed most of the people of Iraq, live in the Tigris-Euphrates valley. They dwell mainly in villages and towns along the river banks, but as elsewhere in the Middle East there is a growing trend toward urbanization. Baghdad, the capital, has a population of about 1.8 million out of a total population in Iraq of just over 11 million. The next largest cities, Basrah and Mosul, number about 420,000 and 340,000.

Religion is a major divisive element. From 52 to 55 percent of the population is Shi'a Muslim, compared to about 35 to 38 percent Sunni Muslim. About 10 percent are non-Muslim: mostly Christians, some Yazidis and pre-Christian Mandeans, and now only a handful of Jews. The Shi'as, which include about three-fourths of the Arab population plus some Persian elements, live mainly in southern Iraq. They are generally on the lower rungs of the scale in Iraqi society, being more rural and less educated than the Sunnis. The latter are predominant among the Arab population north of Baghdad, and among the Kurds and the Bedouins in the west. The Sunni Arabs have always monopolized political power in Iraq and continue to do so under the Ba'thi regime.

Because of the ethnic and religious cleavages, any regime faces the problem of how to get a nationwide consensus of legitimacy. The Kurds are not Arabs and strive to maintain a separate identity. Though Sunnis, they are more militant in their opposition to the Sunni Arab government in Baghdad than their eastern kinsmen are to the Shi'a Persian government in Tehran. And among the Iraqi Arabs, where the Sunnis, though politically strong, are in the minority, many Arab Shi'as have close ties with Shi'a Iran.

Saudi Arabia

Saudi Arabia is one of the more homogeneous gulf states, but even it has noticeable regional differences. The entire population is Arab.[3] Most are Sunnis, and most of the Sunnis are followers of the religious teachings of Muhammad Abd al-Wahhab, the great eighteenth century Najdi revivalist whose name has been given to his followers, the Wahhabis.[4] The Wahhabis subscribe to the most conservative of the four Sunni schools of Islamic jurisprudence, the Hanbali school.

The impact of Islam on Saudi society is all embracing, even with the growing secularization brought about by economic and social development. Islamic law is the law of the land and is practiced in the courts. Time is still often computed by the sun to facilitate the Muslim cycle of five prayers daily (the day begins at sunset, the time of which varies each day). The Muslim lunar calendar is used because it marks Muslim holy days, particularly the annual *hajj* ("pilgrimage") to Mecca which absorbs the energies of nearly everyone in the kingdom for about two months a year. Compliance with religious requirements is enforced by a religious police force, the Mutawwa'in; women are still veiled; and practices and institutions which are considered immoral (e.g., alcohol and public cinemas) are forbidden. There is public radio and television in Saudi Arabia. However, to dispel religious opposition to such innovations, large portions of the programming are devoted to prayers, religious instruction, and readings from the Quran.

Wahhabism has also come to serve as a political ideology for the Saudi state. Since the time when Abd al-Wahhab gained as his patron Muhammad bin Saud, founder of the present Saudi royal family, the Al Saud Wahhabism has given a sense of purpose to generations of Sauds as they united the warring, disparate tribes and principalities of Arabia into present day Saudi Arabia.

Saudi Arabia's 4 million or so inhabitants[5] are fairly evenly divided among city and large-town dwellers and villagers of the oases and the mountains of Hijaz and Asir. Desert nomads, once a powerful political force, are on the decline. Despite the trend towards urbanization, Saudi Arabia has no great metropolis like Baghdad or Tehran. The three largest cities in the kingdom, Riyadh, Jidda, and Mecca, have populations of less than 500,000.

Najd is the political and cultural as well as geographical heartland of Saudi Arabia. Its inhabitants, long insulated from the outside world by the deserts which surround its oasis villages, consider themselves the only racially "pure" Arabs. Unlike the Persian aristocracy, which is distinguished by a regal manner, these desert aristocrats wear their lineage simply, so secure in the superiority of their blood lines that they scarcely question it. Though aristocratic, the Najdis possess a built-in internal egalitarianism. Until his death King Faysal held a weekly open court in which any citizen could petition him, and tribesmen, not recognizing any superiority of the Al Saud blood line, have been known to address him, "ya, Faysal"—"hey Faysal." The great Najdi families are found at all levels of Saudi government and are increasingly involved in business. They are second in importance only to the royal family and to the descendants of Abd al-Wahhab, the Al al-Shaykh who dominates Saudi religious leadership.

Equally important for Najdi attitudes is that, except for a brief period (1818-1822), they have never suffered the psychological scars of foreign invasion or domination.

The Hijaz has traditionally been one of the most polyglot societies in the world, due to the annual influx over the centuries of pilgrims to Mecca and al-Medinah, the two most holy cities in Islam. It was six years after he had conquered the Kingdom of Hijaz in 1926 before King Abd al-Aziz, known to the West as Ibn Saud, risked the degenerative influence of the Hijaz on his Najdi puritans by creating the united Kingdom of Saudi Arabia. Because of its more cosmopolitan outlook, the Hijaz has supplied the kingdom with many of its leading businessmen, soldiers, and technocrats. Its less insular atmosphere has also made many Hijazis somewhat impatient of the political structure dominated by Najdi aristocrats.

The Asir Mountains south of the Hijaz comprise one of the least developed, most densely populated and scenic areas in the country. The isolation of the region, however, is beginning to disappear, as new roads and airports open up the countryside. Asiri men are highly industrious, not refusing manual labor as many Najdis do; and the Qahhabi revival still has not induced many Asiri women to don the veil.

The eastern province of Saudi Arabia is sociologically amorphous. Before the discovery of oil, its population of oasis farmers, fishermen, and mariners was a mixture of Shi'a Arabs, similar to southern Iraqis, and Sunni Arabs, who migrated or claimed to have migrated from the aristocratic tribes of Najd. Since the development of the oil industry, however, the region has seen the influx of people from all over Saudi Arabia and, indeed, all over the Middle East and the West as well. The Saudi oil company employees living in suburbs in Dammam and al-Khubar are as thoroughly middle class as any work force in the world, and centuries in time from the oasis farmers of nearby Qatif Oasis.

Kuwait

The population of Kuwait is estimated to be nearing 1 million, the vast majority living in Kuwait City and its suburbs; over half of the population are aliens.6 The original town of Kuwait (the word is the diminutive of *kut*, or "fort") was founded by clans from the great Najdi tribal confederation, the Anayzah. These clans, who migrated from Najd in the late seventeenth and early eighteenth centuries to escape the continuing famine and tribal warfare of that period, were called the Bani Utub, "the people who migrated."

They discovered the site of present-day Kuwait in 1716, and because there was fresh water, they settled there. Kuwait also offered a safe anchorage, and by the middle of the century, most Kuwaitis had turned to the sea for their livelihood—the beginning of the great Kuwaiti dhow fleets. Though the local accounts imply that Kuwait was uninhabited in 1716, fresh water and a safe anchorage are rare commodities in the gulf, and it is more likely that the Bani Utub displaced or perhaps conquered an older indigenous population. Indeed, nearby archeological sites date back to the third millenium B.C., and a thriving city-state existed earlier on Failaka Island, near Kuwait City. (During his eastern conquest, Alexander the Great renamed Failaka Ikaros.) The town of Kazimah, near the present town of Jahra, was also important during early Muslim times.

The first-ranking clan, the Al-Sabah, became recognized as the leading family by the 1750s and has been the ruling family to this day. The Kuwaitis maintained ties with the tribal interior, and it was in Kuwait that the father and grandfather of Saudi Arabia's King Khalid sought refuge in exile in the latter part of the nineteenth century.

The non-Kuwaiti population is almost entirely a result of the oil industry. Roughly two-thirds of the labor force are foreigners. Mostly from other Arab states, they also include Iranians, Pakistanis, Indians, and other nationalities who came to provide the manpower and technical services which the new oil-based economy required and which the local population was unable to provide. The largest minority group are the Palestinians, variously estimated at around 200,000.

Whereas the aliens have no political rights, they reap many of the benefits of Kuwait's cradle-to-grave welfare system and receive relatively high wages. Thus far they have shown little inclination to agitate for more political representation. This, however, may change in the long run. Originally, the foreign workers were almost always males who left their families behind while seeking to make the family fortune. As the years go by, however, a greater proportion of aliens are residing with their families in Kuwait; and their children, while not Kuwaiti, know no other homeland. Unless the right of citizenship becomes more attainable, this in time may cause future generations of Kuwaiti-born aliens to be more insistent in demanding participation in the political process.

Bahrain

The ruling al-Khalifah family of Bahrain also claims descent from the Bani Utub. In the 1760s several Bani Utub clans left Kuwait and, after traveling south, settled on the tip of the Qatar Peninsula. There they founded a pearl-diving city-state at Zubarah. In 1783-1785 they moved to the Bahrain archipelago, where they imposed a Sunni merchant aristocracy over the predominantly Shi'a oasis farmers and pearl divers there.

Thus, like Iraq, Bahrain has a confessional split between Shi'as and Sunnis. The Shi'a community, which has a slight majority, includes several groups. There are the indigenous inhabitants, called Baharnah, who according to legend were Arabs taken captive by King Nebuchadnezzar and who later escaped and settled in Bahrain. In addition, there are many Shi'as of Iranian origin and some of Saudi and Iraqi origin. Among the Sunnis are the royal family, the Bani Utub aristocracy, and some merchant families from southern Iran, the so-called Lingawis. Some of the latter could possibly have been Shi'as, but for political and economic reasons claim to be Sunnis. There are also Sunnis who, claiming to be *muhawalah*, or "returners," say their families emigrated to the eastern shore of the gulf centuries ago and have now returned.

Indeed, Bahrain has close historical ties with Iran, which has held sovereignty over the archipelago at various times in the past and did not finally relinquish its claims to the islands until 1970. There are generally four types of Iranians in Bahrain and throughout the lower gulf: Shi'a Arabic speakers from Khuzistan; Sunni Arabic speakers from the Lingah area; Baluchis from Kirman and Baluchistan who are employed in manual labor; and Persian speakers from Fars, sometimes called "Red Iranians." Some have been on the Arab side of the gulf for generations, like the Kanoo and Fakhroo families. Most of the Farsi Iranians are merchants and relative newcomers. At any rate, Farsi can be heard in the *suqs* of Manama, the capital, along with Arabic.[7]

Unlike the situation in Kuwait and the lower gulf, a majority of the workforce are native Bahrainis. Because the oil industry was established in Bahrain relatively early, in the early thirties, the country has the largest and most sophisticated native labor force of all the gulf amirates except Kuwait.[8] Bahrain, however, may soon experience a large influx of foreign labor. New projects such as the dry dock now under construction will probably create more jobs than local Bahrainis can fill.

Qatar

Until its oil production first went on stream in 1949, Qatar was a sparsely populated backwater. Its capital, Doha, was little more than a large fishing and pearling village. The native population is mainly Sunni Arab with an admixture of Sunnis from southern Iran. Like their neighbors in Saudi Arabia, native Qataris subscribe to the teaching of the Wahhabi revival and to the Hanbali school of Sunni Islam.

The ascendancy of the ruling Al Thani family dates from the middle of the nineteenth century. Estimated to number in the thousands, it is probably the largest royal family in the gulf. Not only does it constitute the elite of the country, it also comprises a significant proportion of the native Qatari population. That the Al Thanis are not considered to have the aristocratic Arab blood lines of the Bahraini, Kuwaiti, or Saudi royal houses is occasionally a source of irritation, particularly in relations with Bahrain. However, the Al Thanis are the only Muslim ruling house outside of Saudi Arabia who are Wahhabis, and while the Qataris do not adhere to the revivalist teachings as closely as do the Saudis, a common religious bond has enhanced good relations between the two countries.

Next in line to the Al Thani family are the leading Doha merchants. Most are native Qataris, but one of the most powerful families, the Abdallah Darwish, is of southern Iranian origin. The lesser Doha merchants are to a large degree more recent arrivals from Iran, and Farsi can be heard as much as Arabic in the *suqs*. The very few inhabitants of Qatar who live outside the capital are mainly found in scattered fishing villages. Inland, most of the Qatar Peninsula is so barren that the number of pastoral nomads has never been great.

The native population of Qatar is increasingly outnumbered by foreign workers who were drawn by the oil boom. There is a relatively large Palestinian population—mostly clerks and office workers—and there are some Omanis and Yemenis, particularly in the security services, but most of the foreigners are non-Arab. They come mainly from Iran, Pakistan, and India. The Iranians, as in Bahrain, are Arabic speakers from Khuzistan and southern Iran, some of whom have been in Doha for several generations; Farsi merchants; and Baluchis, most of whom are single males engaged in manual labor. Urdu speaking Pakistanis are numerous as lower government employees and clerks and in other petit bourgeois positions, as are the Indians.

All told, the foreign labor force in Qatar is not so permanent as it is in Kuwait. For one thing, the amenities are fewer in Qatar. At the lower end of the labor force, workers typically come for several years, live very frugally, sometimes in rude dormitory conditions, and return home again when they have saved up some capital.

The United Arab Emirates (UAE)

The UAE, historically associated with Oman to the south, is a loose confederation of seven individual shaykhdoms which, before independence in 1971, comprised the Trucial States: Abu Dhabi, Dubai, Sharjah, Ajman, Umm al-Qaywayn, Ras al-Khaymah, and Fujayrah. The origins of these shaykhdoms are all tribal. Six principal tribal groups inhabit the area: the Bani Yas, a confederation of tribes of differing histories and origins; the Manasir (singular: Mansuri), a nomadic tribe which ranges into Saudi Arabia and Qatar; the Qawasim (singular: Qasimi), which has historically been paramount in the northeast; the Ali, or Al Bu Ali; the Sharqiyin (singular: Sharqi); and the Nu'aym, or Na'im (singular: Nu'aymi, or Na'imi).

Most of the Bani Yas are nomads, but by the late 1760s some of them had founded the town of Abu Dhabi as a pearling and fishing center. The head of the paramount branch of the tribe, the Al Bu Falah, settled in Abu Dhabi in the 1790s, and the current ruling family, the Al Nuhayyan, comes from this branch. Another branch, the Al Bu Falasah, settled Dubai, which by 1833 had become an independent and rival city-state, if the term *city* can be applied to a mud-brick village.

The Qawasim, further up the coast, have a proud history of controlling at one time areas on both sides of the gulf. On the Iranian side they were suzerain to the Persian shahs in a manner somewhat analagous to the Norman kings of England who were also dukes of Normandy. This duality is one factor in the territorial dispute over three gulf islands claimed by Iran and two UAE shaykhdoms, Sharjah and Ras al-Khaymah, both of which have Qasimi rulers.9 These proud Qasimi rulers find it difficult to accept handouts from oil-rich Abu Dhabi or Dubai, or to take a subordinate role in UAE affairs. Sharjah's lot may change now that it has become an oil producer.

There is a Qasimi majority in Sharjah, but in Ras al-Khaymah the Qawasim are outnumbered by the fierce, non-Arabic-speaking Shihuh, the Za'b, the Ali, and other tribes. The Ali is also the principal tribe of Umm al-Qaywayn, which is ruled by one of their number. Ajman is ruled by a member of the Al Bu Kharayban branch of the Nu'aym tribe. And in Fujayrah, a Sharqi is shaykh.

Until very recent times, tribal warfare and violence characterized relations among the UAE shaykhdoms, and few rulers died in bed. Even today a map of the country looks like a patchwork quilt, reflecting allegiances of noncontiguous tribal areas to various shaykhs. Several shaykhdoms were at various times subject to other shaykhdoms. One, Kalba, now a part of Sharjah, was at one time independent.

The Wahhabi revival, riding the crest of Saudi political expansion, reached the frontiers of Oman proper in the nineteenth century and has retained adherents to this day. Followers of the Wahhabi school are to be found in the Buraymi Oasis, which is coadministered by Abu Dhabi and Oman and was also claimed by Saudi Arabia until 1974; the Ali tribe of Umm al Qaywayn is also Wahhabi. For these tribesmen, as well as for the Al Thani in Qatar, there is an affinity with their coreligionists in Saudi Arabia. All other Sunnis in the UAE follow the Maliki school (as did most Sunni gulf Arabs before the Wahhabi revival), except the al-Sharqiyin of Fujayrah, who follow the Shafi'i school.

Of all the UAE shaykhdoms only Dubai and Sharjah have developed an extensive *entrepôt* trade and merchant class, although Abu Dhabi merchants are beginning to catch up. Sharjah was the commercial center of the lower gulf until the late 1940s when its "creek" (most lower gulf coastal towns have a creek or estuary which forms a natural harbor) began to silt up.

At the same time the British, partially for political reasons, dredged Dubai's creek, and in time Dubai became the predominant trading center and remains so today. In fact, Dubai, more nearly than anywhere else in the world, is principally a merchant state, and its ruler, a merchant prince, is far more interested in commerce than in politics.

A high proportion of the merchant families of Dubai and Sharjah, as well as of the other UAE shaykhdoms, are foreigners, mainly from Iran, Pakistan, and India. Many have been resident there for generations. Concentrated in the oil-rich shaykhdoms, foreigners also dominate the labor force. These workers, too, are predominantly Iranians, Pakistanis, and Indians. A great proportion of them are Baluchis and Pathans, who perform much of the heavy manual labor. Most of the foreign workers have left family behind and expect to return to their homelands.

Although all the Gulf shaykhdoms have illegal aliens, the UAE probably has the greatest proportion of them. In one way, the illegal aliens aid the government in maintaining security, for they are not apt to make demands and are easy to deport. In the last decade, the number of foreign workers in the UAE has climbed steadily so that foreigners could soon reach as high as two-thirds of the population.

Oman

Oman is the only Arab state whose population is predominantly Ibadi Muslim. Until the accession of the present sultan in 1970, it was for the most part cut off from the outside world. The Omani society is basically tribal and Arab (about seven-eighths), but there is a sizable non-Arab population in the twin-city capital area of Muscat-Mutrah, comprised mostly of Iranians, Pakistanis, and Indians. All of the leading merchants of the country are located in the capital area. Most of the Omani merchants are Ibadi; there are also many foreign merchants including Liwatis (Shi'a Muslims from India) and three important Hindu families.

As mentioned above, Oman has a large Baluchi community. Omani ties with Baluchistan date back to the eighteenth century, when Oman was a regional maritime power. The last of its far-flung empire, which once included Zanzibar in East Africa, was an enclave on the coast of Pakistani Baluchistan, Gwadur, which Oman ceded to Pakistan in 1958 for $8.4 million.

There are two tribal non-Arab groups in Oman, the wild Shihuh who inhabit the Musandam Peninsula (some say they are descended from the Shuhites mentioned in Job), and the Qaras of the Qara Mountains in Dhufar. Both are nominally Sunni Muslim.

There is also a large African population, descendants of former slaves. Slavery has only recently been abolished in Oman. Offensive as the practice might seem in Western eyes, the Arab institution of slavery was not so inhumane as slavery in the West. Slaves had status, acquired from their owners, and were far superior to free men with no status. Perhaps the most inhumane part of the practice was the conditions under which slaves were shipped to Oman from Africa. During the voyage, most of them died. At present, to make amends to the former slaves, the government has adopted policies that make them one of the most pampered groups in the country.

The foreign Muslims are either Shi'as (Iranians and Liwati Indians) or Sunnis (Baluchis, Pakistanis, and Indians). The two Arab tribal groups in Dhufar, the Kathiris and Mahras, are also nominally Sunnis. These two groups have strong tribal ties with neighboring South Yemen. Most of the remaining Arab population, which comprises the bulk of the population, is Ibadi. One of the basic tenets of Ibadi Islam was the selection of an imam rather than hereditary succession. In the middle of the eighteenth century the present ruling family, the Al Bu Said, succeeded in maintaining hereditary succession. The family moved its capital from Nizwa in the interior to Muscat on the coast, and thereafter, there was periodic war between the Al Bu Said and tribes in the interior who continued to support an elected imam. The last such flare-up occurred in 1955, when a British-led force in the name of the sultan ousted the imam from his inland stronghold at Nizwa. The imam has been in exile in Saudi Arabia and Egypt ever since, but is reportedly willing to return home as a nonpolitical figure if the right import dealership can be given to him.

Only in Oman is the ancient division of the northern and southern Arab tribes still a political factor. The southern Arabs, or Qahtanis, according to legend are descended from Himyar, the son of Qahtan, and are called "true Arabs." The northerners, or Adnanis, are said to be descendants of Ibrahim (Abraham) and Ismail (Ishmael) through Adnan, and are called "assimilated Arabs." Elsewhere, the universalism of Islam had long overshadowed the split which had been a principal element in the tribal wars of the

Arabian Peninsula. In Oman, the split is still reflected in the major tribal factions, the Hinawis and the Ghafiris. The labels date from an eighteenth century civil war that pitted the chief of the Bani Hina against the chief of the Bani Ghafir. The Ghafiris attracted the northern Arab tribes while the Hinawis generally attracted the southern Arabs. The Hinawis were the staunchest supporters of the imam. The Ghafiris, among them the Al Bu Said, also are generally Ibadi, but are less strict and more receptive to outside influences. Some of the Ghafiri tribes are Sunni, and a few have adopted the Wahhabi revival.

One other group of Omanis is worth mentioning, the "overseas Omanis." During the years of imamate-sultanate civil strife and the long years of isolation imposed by the present sultan's father, an estimated quarter-million Omanis left the country to find work elsewhere. In addition, the Arab ruling class of Zanzibar, which was historically Omani, was displaced in a revolution in the 1960s. Many of these overseas Omanis have valuable skills desperately needed in Oman. Some, particularly Zanzabaris (many of whom know no Arabic), have returned. Others are more hesitant to do so. Their return would add a tremendous modernizing force to Oman. It has already been noted that returning Omanis with superior skills can create animosities among the less well educated natives. At this juncture, however, Oman can use all the help it can get.

In sum, the gulf is a polyglot of many kinds of people, cultures, and life styles. Much attention has been given in this chapter to tribal, religious, and national affiliations and loyalties. In concluding, however, it should be emphasized that these loyalties are not necessarily, or even frequently, consciously considered by gulf leaders in deciding on policies. No one will say, because I am a Shi'a, or a Wahhabi, or an Arab, or a member of the Bani Utub, I will do thus and so. The gulf leaders head sovereign states, and it is the interests of their states on which they focus in making decisions. But those interests are seen through the eyes of individuals whose own identities are, whether consciously or not, bound up in more traditional loyalties.

NOTES

[1]Carlton S. Coon, *Caravan: The Story of the Middle East,* Rev. Ed. (New York: Henry Holt and Company, 1958), p. 10.

[2]*Ibid.,* p. 11.

[3]There is a small community of central Asian Muslims locally called "Taskhandis" who were allowed to settle after fleeing from the Soviet Union several decades ago.

[4]Wahhabis prefer to be called *Muwahhidin* or "unitarians," denoting their strict monotheism, rather than Wahhabis, which to them implies deification of their spiritual founder. In their strict belief that religious reverence be reserved only for God, Wahhabis are buried in unmarked graves so that no one may come to revere the dead. This applies to kings and commoners alike.

[5]Although there was a census in the early 1960s, no figures were ever released, and estimates vary from 4 to over 8 million. The 1973 United Nations estimate was 8,443,006. Preliminary indications from the 1974 census put the figure close to 4 million.

[6]Population figures in 1970 gave the total population at 738,662, of which 347,396 were aliens and 391,266 were Kuwaiti citizens.

[7]For a more detailed discussion of ethnic groups in the gulf amirates, see John Duke Anthony, *The Arab Gulf Shaykhdoms: People, Politics, Petroleum* (Washington, D.C.: Middle East Institute, 1975).

[8]The terms *shaykh* and *shaykhdom, amir* and *amirate* are used interchangeably in describing the gulf principalities.

[9]See below, Chap. 2, p. 39.

2

The Political Dynamics of the Gulf States

The politics of the gulf operate on several different levels. At one level are the political dynamics of each individual state. At a broader level are the regional gulf politics. And finally, there is the political impact of the gulf on states outside the region, i.e., the gulf in world politics. An understanding of all three levels is essential to a meaningful discussion of U.S. interests in the gulf. This chapter concentrates on the first level, the political dynamics of the separate states.

All gulf political regimes, whether radical or conservative, must operate with roughly the same raw materials: traditional societies and a small but growing number of educated elites. Thus, tribal, family, and technocratic relationships are as important in the operation of government in Ba'thist Iraq as in Wahhabi Saudi Arabia. Another common factor among all the gulf states is a shortage of qualified participants in the governmental decision-making process. Since the gulf area became a principal capital market, this problem has been exacerbated by the large number of foreign visitors who make demands on the time of the small number of key decision makers. Often pressing decisions are delayed simply because no one has time to focus on the problem.

Modern political ideologies play a relatively minor role in domestic Middle Eastern politics. Political actions are based more on personalities than on abstract political ideas. For example, Nasserism, once thought to be the most potent political ideology in the Arab world, did not long survive the leader after whom it was named. Even Ba'thism, which has survived the overthrow of a number of regimes professing to be Ba'thist, is essentially what the various leaders in power say it is. At the moment, there is more enmity between Syrian and Iraqi Ba'thist regimes than between them and several non-Ba'thist regimes.

The political ideology espoused by a regime may, however, give an indication of the country's foreign policy alignment. Radical regimes such as Iraq generally, though not always, side politically with communist countries, and conservative regimes such as Saudi Arabia and Iran side with the West. But this tells one very little about domestic politics. For that, one must look at the relationship between leaders and followers.

Iran

In theory, Iran is a constitutional monarchy with the shah as head of state, a cabinet government headed by a prime minister appointed by the shah, and a two-house legislature. The lower house, the Majlis, consisting of 220 members, is elected by popular universal suffrage. Though Shi'a Islam is the offical state religion, by special provision two Majlis deputies are elected by the Armenian Christian community, and one each by the Zoroastrian (the pre-Islamic faith of Persia) and the Jewish communities. Since 1963, women may also be deputies, and in 1967 four were seated.[1] There is also an upper house, the Senate, generally assigned a lesser role than the Majlis. Half of its sixty members are elected and the other half are appointed by the shah; they all must be Muslim and at least forty years of age. Iran also has an independent judiciary with a legal code based on the French system.

In practice, the present shah dominates the Iranian government, both by his control over the levers of political power and coercion and by the sheer force of his personality. The latter should not be underestimated. The shah was nearly ousted in August 1953 as the result of an abortive attempt by Premier Muhammad Mussadiq to gain control of the country. Since that time, he has steadily increased his personal authority as well as the power and prestige of Iran throughout the region. The energy crisis beginning in 1973 has to some extent given the shah the chance to play a global role. It afforded him a forum, the Organization of Petroleum Exporting Countries (OPEC), and an issue, the world price of oil. With his extraordinary diplomatic talents, he has used the oil issue to project a forceful image of power. As one long-time observer of Iranian affairs stated it, the shah is about the closest thing to an absolute monarch existing in the world today.

The shah governs through a complex network of informal, interlocking, and sometimes competing personal relationships. For example, often two cabinet ministers are asked to provide the same information or undertake the same task: in this way, the shah can safeguard against unreliable information from an official who is "putting a good face" on unpleasant news, or can create incentive through competition to get a task done as quickly and efficiently as possible. Knowing how to function within the governmental system (or for an outsider, knowing how to insure that it functions for him) therefore entails much more than merely knowing who fills what position. In many cases, one's position of influence within the informal system can be more important than the formal position or job title one holds. This, of course, also holds true for most of the gulf states.

The political security of the regime rests on the internal security and national defense forces, on the one hand, and an ambitious economic development program, the White Revolution, on the other. The White Revolution is actually a continuation of the shah's basic development program, first announced in the Land Reform Bill of 1962. Even the most cursory look at Iranian government expenditures will show how much importance the shah places on both security and development.

The shah's technocratic absolutism supercedes the older traditional system of political dynamics in which tribal, religious, commercial, and other groups participated in the distribution power. While these groups are still economically and socially very important in many respects, the consolidation of physical and economic power by the shah through the bureaucracy and armed and security forces has eliminated most of their participation in the political system.

The process has also resulted in modernization and social reform being imposed from above, which is perhaps the only way it can be effective. This has been a positive factor in that the government can override parochial interests resisting change. But it also in some cases limits the real depth of change, creating instead a facade under which traditional ideas are still very strong and bitterness and frustration remain barely beneath the surface.

Iraq

Iraq has a single-party regime under the Socialist Arab Ba'th ("Renaissance") party. The government is a branch of the same party that rules Syria, but the two regimes are not on good terms, each claiming orthodoxy with the zeal characteristic of revolutionaries. Like many revolutionary ideologies in the Middle East, Ba'thism is an imprecise amalgamation of antiimperialistic xenophobia, nostaliga for the golden age of the Arab caliphates, and a strong commitment to redistribution of wealth and power for the benefit of the poorer classes. Its major appeal in Iraq has been among the city dwellers at the lowest and least secure end of the middle class.

As in many one-party states where party membership is a *sine qua non* for career advancement, many younger Iraqis of all socially and politically aware classes are joining the Ba'th party. However, if one considers only the party's politically committed members, it represents a small minority of the population. Despite this, no anti-Ba'thi group has the capability to overthrow the regime, and the government is careful to maintain the loyalty of the army, which does have the resources to effect a coup. By Middle East standards, the Ba'th regime in Iraq is relatively stable.

The Ba'th party of Iraq has two wings, a military wing which at the time of this writing is led by Iraqi President Ahmad Hasan al-Bakr, and a civilian wing headed by Saddam Husayn al-Tikriti, vice chairman of the party and of the Revolutionary Command Council.[2] President Bakr is considered the elder statesman of the regime, but in recent years he has taken an increasingly less active role in politics. The civilian wing of the party, under Saddam Husayn, has become ascendant and currently dominates Iraqi politics.

Saddam Husayn has a reputation for ruthless pragmatism. To Western eyes, the combination may seem a bit perplexing. He has never allowed Ba'th ideology, however defined, to interfere with meeting the needs and interests of Iraq as he perceives them. At the same time, however, recent signs that Iraq may be moderating its hostility to the West should not be interpreted as a relinquishing of the radical, revolutionary spirit inherent in Ba'thism.

In recent years, despite strong foreign policy concerns over the Arab-Israeli problem, Arab world politics, Iran, and the Persian Gulf, Iraq has tended to focus primarily on domestic issues. Until the Iranian-Iraqi rapprochement announced on March 6, 1975, the most pressing problem was the Kurdish insurgency aided by Iran. As a result of the rapprochement, the situation now appears to be manageable, but the Kurdish national movement in both Iraq and Iran will continue to be a major potential security problem.

From the Iraqi regime's point of view, much needs to be done in economic development and in extending its base of support throughout the country. With vastly increased revenues accruing from higher oil prices, domestic development is going on at an accelerated pace. The effects of this development on the political dynamics of Iraq remain to be seen, but over time they are almost certain to be far-reaching.

Saudi Arabia

The kingdom of Saudi Arabia was created in 1932 from the formerly separate principalities of Najd and the Hijaz. Members of the House of Saud have ruled over Najd, however, since the mid-eighteenth century, except for periods when rivals temporarily eclipsed them. In 1818, for example, an Ottoman army invaded and burned the Saudi capital, Dir'iyya. The Sauds rebuilt their capital nearby at Riyadh, where it has remained to this day.

Saudi Arabia is one of the very few countries for which sacred Islamic, or Shari'a, law forms the fundamental law of the land. The judicial system is based on Islamic courts presided over by *qadis,* Islamic judges. Because according to the Shari'a only God can make laws, there has been no legislature in Saudi Arabia in the Western sense. The equivalent of Western legislation has taken the form of administrative regulations called *nizams.* There is, however, a practically defunct Consultative Assembly (Majlis al-Shurra) for the Hijaz, and in April 1975 Crown Prince Fahd announced plans to create a national Consulative Assembly.[3]

The king of Saudi Arabia is the chief of state and head of government. Saudi public administration did not evolve according to a master plan. Instead, institutions were created as the need for them arose. The first national ministry was Foreign Affairs, established in 1930, when the country was still the Kingdom of the Hijaz and Najd. Except for one brief period, King Faysal was foreign minister from the creation of the ministry until his death in 1975. In the last years of King Faysal's reign, however, much of the day to day conduct of foreign affairs was delegated to the late Omar al-Saqqaf (d. 1974), who was given the title minister of state for foreign affairs. Under King Khalid, Faysal's son Prince Saud has been appointed minister of foreign affairs.

The Ministry of Finance was founded in 1932 and many of the subsequent ministries began as departments under it. The most recent ministry, Justice, was formed in 1970. Under the new administration of King Khalid and Crown Prince Fahd, other changes, particularly in local government, can be expected.

The development of the Saudi bureaucracy has channeled political power into a more organized and regulated administrative system than was the case under the traditional system of personal consultation practiced by the king's father, Abd al-Aziz. Nevertheless, the functioning of the bureaucracy still has many holdovers from the traditional system. Ministries often operate independently of each other; delegation of authority is at best limited; and decision making is still highly personalized.

The king is at the apex of the Saudi political system. But since the accession of King Khalid after the assassination of King Faysal on March 25, 1975, a new element has been added. Khalid as king and prime minister must ultimately be responsible for all decisions. But his half-brother Crown Prince Fahd has been given the role of chief administrator of the government. (There is a precedent for this kind of situation in the late 1950s, when Faysal, then crown prince, was prime minister under his brother King Saud.) At the time of this writing it is still too early to tell what effect the dual Khalid-Fahd administration will have on Saudi decision making.

Because the Saudi king is supreme in national politics, it has been widely assumed in the West that he is an absolute monarch. This is not so. Shari'a law places definite constraints on the king's powers. More important, the king is answerable to the royal family, without whose support he cannot rule. Saudi royal-family politics operate completely outside the framework of Saudi national politics, although many prominent royal princes are also active in national politics.

Numbering from 3,000 to 7,000, the House of Saud is very circumspect about its affairs and little is known about its dynamics. The most powerful group are the sons of Abd al-Aziz, from whose number the past three kings and present crown prince were chosen. The sons tend to gravitate toward sibling groups of full brothers (King Abd al-Aziz had many wives). The senior brother, Prince Muhammad, is also a full brother of King Khalid. Because of health and personal reasons, Muhammad chose to give up his claims to the throne in favor of a younger brother. One of the most powerful sibling groups is the seven-member Al Fahd ("Family of Fahd," named for the eldest brother; the group is also known in the West as the Sudayri Seven, after the maiden name of their mother). Of the seven, Fahd is crown prince, first deputy prime minister, and minister of interior; Sultan is minister of defense and aviation; Naif is minister of state for interior; and three others have noncabinet positions in the government.

Other important groups within the royal family are the surviving brothers of Abd al-Aziz. Prince Abdullah bin Abd al-Rahman, the eldest surviving uncle of King Khalid, is the senior member of the family. Prince Musa'd, the former minister of finance and national economy, is another. In addition to the immediate family, there are three important collateral branches: the Bin Jaluwis, the Thunayans, and the Al Saud al-Kabirs. King Khalid's mother was a Bin Jaluwi, as is the amir ("governor") of Eastern Province. Because it is descended from an older brother of King Abd al-Aziz's father, the Saud al-Kabir branch actually claims precedence over all but the king in royal family protocol. All members of the royal family, plus leading religious figures (including the Al al-Shaykhs, descendants of founder of Wahhabism) and cabinet-ranking political figures, comprise the *ahl al-aqd wal-hall*, "the people who bind and loose." In 1964 this group deposed King Saud in favor of King Faysal.

Other important groups in Saudi Arabia include the nonroyal Najdi aristocratic families, the leading one of which is the Sudayris. Of somewhat lesser importance politicially are tribal and business leaders. The armed forces have never played the key role in Saudi politics that they have in other developing countries. As a safeguard against a military coup, however, Saudi Arabia has a tribally organized National Guard under Prince Abdallah, another half-brother of the king and second deputy prime minister.

One unique aspect of Saudi public administration is the annual *hajj* ("pilgrimage") to Mecca, attended by a million and a half Muslims. At a cost of millions of dollars a year, the *hajj* requires the entire administrative resources of the government.

It occurs annually according to the Muslim calendar, which is eleven days shorter than the solar calendar. This is one reason (the main reasons are religious) why the Saudis have not adopted a solar fiscal year. They would be too hard pressed to administer the *hajj* and produce the annual budget if both were required in the same period, as would eventually happen. Producing the budget also takes nearly all the administrative resources of the government.

Kuwait

To a large degree, Kuwait and the other gulf amirates are governed as oligarchical partnerships among the ruling families, tribal affiliations, and an old, established merchant class. The terms of these partnerships differ in each case, and the massive inflow of oil revenues is affecting far-reaching changes, but generally speaking, the business of government in these states is primarily business.

Kuwait is a constitutional monarchy with the amir as chief of state, a cabinet government, a National Assembly, and an independent judiciary. The judicial system, while theoretically based on Shari'a law, is in practiced based on a legal code adopted from the Egyptian code, which itself was largely based on European law.

The Al Sabahs, as the royal family, are at the head of the Kuwaiti political system. From their number are chosen the amir, the prime minister, and many of the more important ministers.

Two groups of cousins within the family are important politically, the Al Jabir and the Al Salim. Traditionally the two branches alternated in providing the ruler, but in 1965 Amir Sabah, an Al Salim, succeeded Abdallah, another Al Salim. Since then, attempts have been made to placate the Al Jabirs and their supporters with government appointments at the expense of the Al Salim supporters. Moreover, the crown prince is Shaykh Jabir al-Ahmad, of the Al Jabir branch.

The Al Sabahs have never dominated political decision making in Kuwait the way the Al Sauds have in Saudi Arabia. Traditionally, they shared power with aristocratic merchant families such as the Ghanims, Saqrs, Salihs, Khalids, and Jana'ts. To a great extent, power sharing has been informal. Since the original 1962 Constitution, a National Assembly was established, but it was abolished in August 1976. Although restricted in its legislative authority, the assembly had been more than a rubber stamp, and often took the government to task over various issues. Its dissolution, together with curtailment of freedom of the press, was considered more of a precautionary move by the government than a reaction to perceived abuses. The government feared that the instability generated by the Lebanese civil war might spill over into the gulf and that Kuwait's assembly and free press would be exploited to the detriment of its internal security. In fact, fears for internal stability have led most of the gulf rulers to question in the past few years the appropriateness of legislatures.

Since its inception, the National Assembly has included an opposition group noted for its progressive, leftist views. The "elder statesman" of this group is Dr. Ahmad al-Khatib, head of the Kuwaiti organization of the Marxist-leaning Arab Nationalist movement (ANM). A younger member is Sami Munayyis, editor of *al-Tali'a*. Over the years, the opposition appears to have matured. Although socialisit rhetoric is still constantly heard in the National Assembly, the opposition in recent years has also begun to focus on domestic as well as foreign issues, questioning the way in which Kuwaiti government policies affect the Kuwaiti national interest.

One of the chief restrictions of the National Assembly is its very narrow electoral base. Of a total population of nearly 1 million in Kuwait, less than half are Kuwaiti citizens; and of the latter, only about 50,000 are qualified to vote. The narrow electoral base ensures control of the government by the oligarchical power elite. But it denies participation in the political decision-making process to a growing number of educated and capable young Kuwaitis, who are largely the product of Kuwait's cradle-to-grave welfare program, which includes free education, and there is increasing concern both within and outside the government over how to deal with the problem.

The large number of aliens in Kuwait, including some 200,000 Palestinians, has been viewed by many as a potential source of political instability. But except for the growing number of long-time alien residents who, as nonenfranchised Kuwaitis, wish more participation in the political process, the alien population has not to date been a security threat. This is in part due to the government's policy of co-opting potential dissidents through its generous welfare system, many of the benefits of which are shared with non-Kuwaitis. In addition, wages and the standard of living in Kuwait are far better than most aliens could expect to find at home or elsewhere, and the threat of expulsion for any subversive activity is a considerable deterrent.

The armed forces, though only about 10,000 in number, provide the physical power behind the regime. Their loyalty is therefore quite important. The Kuwaiti armed forces are equipped with the latest equipment, and are relatively well trained and educated. Thus far, the possibility of a dissident officers' movement, though never to be ruled out, has been considered fairly remote.

In sum, the combination of the royal family-merchant family oligarchy, the all-embracing welfare system, and the armed forces has kept Kuwait relatively stable. An additional safety valve should be mentioned: the Kuwait press is among the freest, if not the most free, of any in the entire Middle East.

Bahrain

Fully independent only since 1971, Bahrain elected to follow Kuwait's lead in creating an Islamic constitutional monarchy and an elected National Assembly (Majlis al-Watini). Bahrain's assembly had even fewer powers than Kuwait's, but a far greater proportion of its population (of some 250,000) could vote. In August 1975, however, the assembly was dissolved.

The royal family of Bahrain, the al-Khalifahs, has not had to share power with the merchant aristocracy to the same extent that their royal cousins in Kuwait have. Moreover, the merchant class was not particularly interested in the new National Assembly. Thus, the Bahraini assembly did not mirror the merchant oligarchy in Bahrain. Additionally, despite a fairly large electoral base, the assembly attracted few of the younger educated Bahrainis. This group still gravitates primarily to the government bureaucracy. Government workers had to resign their positions to take a seat in the Majlis, and generally they preferred the security of bureaucracy over the uncertainties of politics.

As a result, the Majlis consisted for the most part of tradition-alists, few of whom had a Western education. Such representation emphasized—perhaps overemphasized—the religious cleavages between the Shi'a and Sunni communities.

Two other groups were represented in the Majlis, labor and the leftist intellectuals; the latter also espouse the cause of the laboring class. In the absence of labor unions, these representatives did provide some means for communication between labor and government. The grand old man of the radicals, Abd al-Aziz Sa'd Shamlan, returned to Bahrain after years of exile and was elected to the 1972 assembly, which was tasked to draft a constitution. In the 1974 elections, however, he failed to obtain a seat. A younger group of radicals were elected, including Dr. Abd al-Hadi Khalaf of the radical National Liberation Front-Bahrain (NLF-B)—it and all other parties are banned—and Yusif Hasan al-Ajaji. However, they and three others were barred by the government from taking their seats. Many in the ruling elite considered the Majlis a haven of radicalism and welcomed its dissolution.

Despite the brief experiment in constitutional monarchy, the al-Khalifahs always monopolized the power structure. Shaykh Isa bin Salman is the ruler, his brother Shaykh Khalifa bin Salman is prime minister, and Shaykh Muhammad bin Mubarak is foreign minister. Several other members of the family also hold important ministerial portfolios. The impetus for governmental reform comes in great part from the ruler, Shaykh Isa. To the extent that reform enhances the feeling of participation among the Bahraini population, it can be viewed as a long-range investment by the royal family in maintaining the regime. Given declining oil revenues, a large labor force, and a sophistication that in the past has spawned a tradition of labor unrest, reform appears very worthwhile and the dissolution of the assembly a setback. In the meantime, Bahrain has to rely on its security forces, which are aided by outside advisors, in order to maintain its internal security.

Qatar

Of all the gulf amirates, the division of labor between the merchant class and the royal family is greatest in Qatar. The ruling Al Thani family has had a virtual monopoly on government, and the business community has stuck pretty largely to business. To be sure, there was and is close cooperation between the two groups for mutual benefit, but each has remained for the most part in its own sphere. That trend is beginning to change, if only slightly. Abundant oil revenues have brought the royal family a more lively interest in business, and the merchant community a more active interest in the repository of those revenues, the government. Moreover, educated young members of both groups are beginning to seek broader horizons than those of their fathers.

For the foreseeable future, nevertheless, the government appears to be firmly in the hands of the royal family. A constitution was adopted in 1970 (before the British departure), creating a Council of Ministers and an independent judiciary based in theory on Islamic law as in Kuwait and Bahrain. Although some mention was made of a Consultative Council, there is no independent legislative branch and laws are made by decree. The ruler, Shaykh Khalifah bin Hamad Al Thani, is also prime minister, and ten of the fifteen ministerial portfolios are held by members of the royal family, including the key ministries of Interior, Defense, Finance and National Economy and Foreign affairs.

Despite the constitution, therefore, the only major constraints on the ruler's power are Islam and the royal family. Shaykh Khalifah, who is known as a forceful and dedicated ruler, ousted his cousin Shaykh Ahmad in 1972 in what is known locally as the Change. There is still some ill feeling between the two branches of the family, but not enough to threaten the security of the regime. The Al Thanis, who subscribe to the Wahhabi revival, are militantly anticommunists and keep a tight rein on potential subversion. Their security forces are among the best in the gulf amirates.

The regime is spending a great deal of its resources on education, social welfare, and economic development projects, and as yet, expectations of the people seem not to have exceeded the government's ability to meet them. The conservatism of the population, the benefits of oil revenues, and strong security measures have thus combined to make Qatar, at least for now, one of the more stable of the gulf amirates. In the longer run, however, much will depend on the regime's capability to adapt to the changing social, economic, and political conditions that its development programs are certain to create.

The United Arab Emirates (UAE)

On December 1, 1971, Britain formally relinquished its protective status over the seven lower gulf shaykhdoms known collectively as the Trucial States. The following day, six of the seven joined a loose federation, the United Arab Emirates (UAE). The seventh, Ras al-Khaymah, did not join until February 10, 1972.

There is almost as much disparity as similarity among the UAE members. None has a large population, but the range among them is fairly wide. Abu Dhabi has the most inhabitants, about 80,000, and Dubai has slightly less; Sharjah's population is around 35,000; Ras al-Khaymah has around 30,000; and Ajman, Umm al-Qaywayn, and Fujayrah all number less than 10,000. They are economically disparate also. Abu Dhabi has a huge oil income; Dubai has both an oil and a mercantile economy; and Sharjah has just come on stream with a modest amount of oil. As yet, Ras al-Khaymah has found no oil, but does have a relatively productive agricultural sector. The other three emirates are desperately poor, subsisting on fishing, nomadic herding, some pearling, and largess from their wealthier neighbors, chiefly Abu Dhabi.

The closest political analogy to the UAE in the West is the United States as it existed under the Articles of the Confederation, when each state retained a large degree of autonomy. The UAE provisional constitution, promulgated in 1971, provides for a president, vice president, Council of Ministers, and a legislative body called the Federal National Council. Of the forty seats in the legislative council, eight each are allotted to Abu Dhabi and Dubai; six each to Sharjah and Ras al-Khaymah; and four each to Ajman, Dubai, and Umm al-Qaywayn. Council members are appointed by their various rulers and meet for six-month sessions beginning in November each year. At the first meeting, in February 1972, a speaker and two deputy speakers were elected. Among the council's responsibilities is approving the budget, and it can also initiate legislation. In fact, however, with power firmly in the hands of the seven rulers, the legislative body is little more than a debating society. The president of the UAE, with the approval of the Federal Supreme Council, can dissolve the Federal National Council by decree.

Institutionally, the real power in the federal structure is vested in the Federal Supreme Council, composed of the shaykhs of the seven member amirates. In some respects this body is the continuation of collegial consultation within the old Trucial States Council, established by the British in 1952. Federal Supreme Council decisions must have the approval of five of the seven members; Abu Dhabi and Dubai have a veto power.

In theory, the UAE federal structure was originally to have control over defense, finance, and foreign affairs, with all internal powers remaining under the local jurisdiction of the various amirates. In practice, the lines of demarcation are much more blurred. Each amirate jealously guards its prerogatives and cooperates within the federal structure only to the extent that its own interests are served or protected.

The success of guiding the UAE through its birth pangs to its current state of development is largely attributed to its president, Shaykh Zayd bin Sultan Al Nuhayyan of Abu Dhabi. Not only does Abu Dhabi contribute the largest proportion of the UAE budget, but the other major contributor, Dubai, has to date never paid its share. Thus the wheels of the UAE turn almost entirely on Abu Dhabi money.

From the outset, the Ministry of Foreign Affairs has acted as the spokesman for the entire UAE in regional and international affairs. Some of the UAE ambassadors abroad, however, retain more loyalty to their amirates than to the union they represent. The Finance Ministry has never had any power, since financial policy is set by the individual shaykhdoms. On the other hand, the central bank, called the UAE Currency Board, does regulate money and banking for the entire federation.

The union's Ministry of National Defense has also not functioned very well. The minister, Shaykh Muhammad bin Rashid al-Maktum, is the son of the ruler of Dubai. The UAE inherited the British-created Trucial Oman Scouts, renamed the Union Defense Force (UDF). Its principal mission is to keep order among the tribes, and, under the British, it remained strictly uninvolved in tribal politics. Although there are still expatriates and representatives from all the shaykhdoms among its officers and men, the UDF's association with Dubai has weakened its nontribal identification. Moreover, the UDF has been eclipsed in size and capability by the Abu Dhabi Defense Force (ADDF). The latter numbers around 6,000 men, including mostly expatriate officers, and is equipped with Mirage aircraft. Shaykh Zayd, in his capacity as president of the UAE, has increasingly called out the ADDF to quell tribal disputes in the other shaykhdoms, often without waiting to consult the local rulers. In addition to the UDF and the ADDF, other shaykhdoms have small internal security forces.

In an effort to again unify the defense forces, all the local forces were united in May 1976. However, the ADDF, now called the Western Military Command, is still the largest and most powerful component of the armed forces.

One of the most successful UAE ministries is Education. It administers schools throughout the amirates, and is expanding the school system as rapidly as possible. In the long run, the federal school system could be a major contributor to political attitudes strengthening the concept of union.

Another unifying factor is the extensive program to link the UAE by an all-weather road system. Already one can drive from Abu Dhabi to Ras al-Khaymah and beyond in under three hours and to the Buraymi Oasis town of al-Ayn in little over an hour. New roads are being planned and constructed into the hinterland, including a road to link the Gulf of Oman coast with the rest of the UAE.

In late 1973 Shaykh Zayd announced measures he was taking to strengthen the federal structure. Basically they consisted of abolishing the Abu Dhabi Council of Ministers and incorporating all but his key ministries (e.g., Finance and Defense) into the UAE cabinet. The latter was increased in size to twenty-six ministries plus the prime minister and a deputy prime minister. In many ways, the larger cabinet is still window dressing in that federal-level decisions are made by the president and the Federal Supreme Council. The expansion did enable Zayd to bring into the cabinet more representatives from the poorer amirates. At the same time, jobs had to be found for the Abu Dhabi ministers whose ministries had been abolished, and some of the new ministries, while federal in name, are in practice still only responsible for Abu Dhabi affairs. A case in point is the elevation of the Abu Dhabi Ministry of Petroleum to the federal level. The other two oil producers, Dubai and Sharjah, not only dictate their own oil policies, but neither of them have ever participated in the

Organization of Petroleum Exporting Countries (OPEC), although The UAE is a member. Thus the UAE minister of petroleum administers only Abu Dhabi oil.

Despite these beginnings of a federal structure, the locus of power in the UAE still rests at the individual shaykhdom level.

Abu Dhabi is the largest, wealthiest, and most powerful of all the amirates. Shaykh Zayd rules as a traditional Islamic monarch, the major constraints being Islam and the royal family. The Al Nuhayyan are the paramount family of the Al Bu Falah branch of the Bani Yas tribe. Not only Al Nuhayyan family politics, but also broader tribal politics, enter into government decision making. Unlike most of the other gulf states, Abu Dhabi never has developed an extensive merchant class.

Before the post-1973 oil boom, Zayd was very accessible to his subjects. The huge demands on his time since then, as both shaykh of Abu Dhabi and president of the UAE, and the shortage of bureaucratic expertise to share some of the burden, have made him far less accessible as time goes on. Though probably not serious, there are grumblings among tribal and other leaders that they can no longer get an audience as they once could.

Abu Dhabi still has some key ministries, as mentioned above. As elsewhere in the gulf, foreign advisors also play a big role. Beyond these groups, public administration is almost nonexistent except for the ADDF and security forces. In 1971 Zayd created a Consultative Council. Numbering fifty, it is entirely appointed by the ruler and has few powers other than helping to create a consensus through which the ruler makes decisions.

Dubai's ruler, Shaykh Rashid al-Maktum, was expected to be a major political personality in the UAE when it was established in 1971. He is vice president of the federation and three of his sons are the UAE prime minister, minister of finance and industry, and minister of national defense. To date, however, Rashid has not concerned himself very actively in federation affairs. His attitude toward the union appears to be ambivalent. While not actively opposed to it, neither does he support it beyond making sure that Dubai's interests do not suffer from his nonparticipation.

Shaykh Rashid is head of the paramount al-Maktum family of the Al Bu Falasa branch of the Bani Yas. He rules Dubai more as the chairman of the board and majority stockholder than as a monarch, and is much more interested in business than in government. While Rashid's authority is clearly supreme, he rules through informal relationships with the merchant-class oligarchy, expatriate advisors, and tribal and other groups. He is extremely accessible and appears to have knowledge, if not a share, of every business enterprise in the amirate.

Public administration in Dubai is haphazard. The ruler depends on a trusted group of people, including a number of expatriates, most of whom have been in Dubai for a very long time. For example, one of his closest advisors is Mahdi Tajir, of Bahraini origin, currently UAE ambassador to London. Such basic areas as public finance, customs, public works, and police functions are also administered in great part through foreign advisors or through foreign banks and companies. One of Dubai's major problems is keeping middle-ranking personnel. One expatriate advisor complained that, because of such low salaries in the public sector, it is too great a temptation for this group, once trained, to leave the government bureaucracy and seek to become millionaires.

Sharjah is just ten miles up the road from Dubai (you can see one town from the other on a clear day). Sharjah has never had good relations with neighboring Dubai, and Sharjawis still remember the days when Sharjah, not Dubai, was the leading commercial center in the lower gulf. The ruler, Shaykh Sultan bin Muhammad al-Qasimi, is the only gulf ruler to have earned a university degree. He came to power in 1972 after an unsuccessful coup resulted in the death of the former ruler, Shaykh Khalid.

In the last year, Sharjah has become an oil producer, giving its economy and its merchant community a new lease on life. While Shaykh Sultan is in close consultation with the merchant community, particularly on economic development policies, tribal politics are also a major consideration in Sharjah's politics, particularly those of the predominant Qawasim tribe, to which the royal family belongs. The shaykh administers several noncontiguous tribal enclaves, including three towns on the Gulf of Oman—Dibba, the jursidiction of which is actually split among Sharjah, Fajayrah, and Oman; Khawr Fakkan; and Kalba, once a separate amirate.

Ras al-Khaymah's royal family is also from the Qawasim. The ruler, Shaykh Saqr bin Muhammad al-Qasimi, is thus related to the ruler of Sharjah, and the two amirates have had a long history of close political association.

Shaykh Saqr is a very dynamic and independent-minded ruler. He chafes under the disability of not possessing an oil income, and his dissatisfaction with the preponderant role of Abu Dhabi and Dubai in the new federation was a major reason he refused to join the UAE for almost three months after its creation.

With only a very small merchant community and a lack of economic development, Saqr's political administration is far more traditionalist, rudimentary, and tribally oriented than the administrations of oil-producing shaykhdoms. In this regard, Ras al-Khaymah is ruled in much the same personal and informal manner as the three poorest and smallest shaykhdoms, *Ajman, Umm al-Qaywayn,* and *Fujayrah.*

Oman

Political dynamics underwent a tremendous change in Oman in 1970 when the present sultan, Qabus bin Said Al Bu Said, replaced his father, Said bin Taymur, in a bloodless coup. Prior to 1970, Said bin Taymur had ruled as an oriental despot, playing off tribes, merchants, and religious groups with the aid of his British-led army. In later years a recluse, he lived in Salalah, capital of Dhufar, 600 miles from the national capital at Muscat. Qabus, who was educated in England, also lived in Salalah under house arrest for the years preceding the coup. Under Said bin Taymur, the country languished, and even after oil production began in 1967, almost no efforts were made to modernize.

One of Sultan Qabus's first acts was to rename the country the Sultanate of Oman. The old name, Muscat and Oman, accentuated the historical political cleavage between inner Oman and the coastal area around the capital. This division had last erupted into open hostilities in the 1950s when a British-led force defeated the Ibadi imam, who fled from his "capital" at Nizwa into exile in Saudi Arabia.

In 1970 Dhufar was also incorporated into Oman. Formerly, it had the status of a separate sultanate joined to Muscat only in the person of the ruler. Qabus had thus unified the country in name. It now remained for him to unify it in fact.

Since 1970, Qabus has instituted a Council of Ministers with seventeen cabinet positions.[4] Local government is administered by forty *walis* ("governors"), and each *wilayah* ("governate" or "province") has attached to it a *qadi*, or Shari'a judge. In the major towns, there are also municipal councils whose members are chosen by the traditional means of tribal affiliation and consensus. Despite these innovations, decision making still emanates from the top. The burgeoning range of decisions to be made as a result of ambitious development programs, the tendency of the sultan to delegate authority only to a few trusted advisors, and the dearth of technocrats able to make decisions all combine to make the governing process more cumbersome in many ways than it was in the past.

The politically important groups in Oman are the royal family, the tribes, the merchant community, and key expatriate advisors. Under Said bin Taymur, an elaborate web of personal relationships was used to deal with these groups, at times playing one group off against the other. Under Sultan Qabus, much of the old system has been dropped, but because the new governmental institutions that the sultan is creating have not been functioning long enough to comprise a new system, political dynamics are for the present in somewhat of a transitional stage. In other words, decision making is still centered at the top and the same groups still have influence, but new lines of communication through the bureaucracy are competing with the old personality network, thus changing the configuration of power.

In the new configuration, the royal family still has a major influence. The sultan relies on his uncles and cousins in key positions in the government, including a number of the ministerial posts. The political power of the tribes appears to be waning. On the other hand, the merchant class is holding its own, but is having to compete with the bureaucracy to participate in economic development projects. The predominance of non-Ibadi, and in many cases non-Omani, merchants may further dilute the influence of this group as Omani nationalism grows. Moreover, oil revenues may also induce Omanis who formerly shunned commerce to compete with the old established families.

The regime continues to rely heavily on expatriates. The British, who maintain their base rights on Masirah Island, still largely run the armed forces. There are British advisors in other key positions as well. Iranian and Jordanian troops have been sent to the sultan to counter the insurgency in Dhufar, and Pakistani officers are seconded to the sultan's navy. The oil company Petroleum Development Oman (PDO), with its foreign management, plays a major role in finance. Many third-country Arabs also have influential advisory positions.

Oman, with its lack of trained manpower and development programs and its still embryonic educational system, will have to rely on expatriates for some time to come. The relationship of foreign advisors to Omanis, however, is changing. For years, the British had what amounted to a *de facto* protective role in Oman. Under Qabus, that has all changed. There is now a distinct feeling that as quickly as possible the Omanis aim to control their own affairs.

NOTES

[1]American University, *Area Handbook for Iran* (Washington, D.C.: The American University, 1971), p. 225.

[2]His official titles are assistant secretary of the Regional Command of the Socialist Arab Ba'th party and deputy chairman of the Revolutionary Command Council of the Iraqi Republic.

[3]"Policy Statement of the Kingdom of Saudi Arabia" (a paid advertisement by the Ministry of Information of Saudi Arabia), *Washington Post,* April 15, 1975, p. A-15.

[4]The sultan at the time of this writing is his own defense and finance ministers.

3
Regional Politics of the Gulf

The Gulf as a Regional Political Arena

Outside interest in the regional politics of the gulf stems mainly from interest in gulf oil. But oil is not the driving force of gulf politics, even though it does play a very important role; the politics of the region are primarily the product of internal relationships. Inherent in these relationships are a number of striking contrasts that on occasion erupt into open confrontations and even hostilities. The greatest contrasts lie among conflicting political ideologies and between the two nationalisms which collide head on in the gulf.

In the previous chapter, it was concluded that all of the political systems in the area work with roughly the same human resources and govern in much the same way. It was also noted that the peoples of the area tend to follow political leaders rather than abstract political ideas or ideologies. Nevertheless, there are distinct ideological differences among the gulf political systems. Iraq in the north and the People's Democratic Republic of Yemen (PDRY of South Yemen) to the southwest of the gulf region have radical regimes. Iran, Saudi Arabia, Kuwait, the gulf amirates, and Oman, despite differences in their political outlook and development, all have basically conservative regimes.

Parts of this chapter were developed and expanded from an earlier essay by the author, "Confrontation and Cooperation in the Gulf," *Middle East Problem Paper* no. 10 (Washington, D.C.: The Middle East Institute, December 1974).

The arena for ideological differences is primarily in the field of foreign affairs, both regionally and in gulf relations with the rest of the world. To a great degree, the political stability of the gulf depends not only on the ability of each regime to cope with internal change, but also on the amount of political tension being generated in the region as a whole. One of the key factors in determining the level of tension is the confrontation of radicalism and conservatism.

The two principal states opposing the spread of radicalism in the gulf are Iran and Saudi Arabia. They are the largest, the most influential and powerful of all the conservative states. Thus, the other conservative states, particularly in the area of security, must depend largely on the political, economic, and military support of these two countries. The peripheral states that also play a role in gulf security are Jordan, which has sent combat troops to Oman and military and public security advisors elsewhere in the gulf; and Pakistan, which has military missions in Saudi Arabia, Oman, and the UAE.

Despite the desire of Iran and Saudi Arabia and the other conservative gulf states to cooperate, particularly in the area of regional security, their capacity to do so is inhibited by the collision of Arab and Persian nationalisms in the gulf. Divided by language, culture, and historical traditions, there has rarely been a great affinity between the Persians and the Arabs. They do share a common religion, but even that is tempered by religious schism. The Iranians are predominantly Shi'a Muslims, while most of the Arabian Peninsula Arabs are Sunnis. The conservative Wahhabi Saudis particularly find some of the Shi'a practices repugnant to their strict interpretation of Islam.

The sense of national consciousness in the lower gulf states has not been as fully developed as it is farther north, but even in the lower gulf it is becoming a major political factor. Shaykhdoms which before 1973 scarcely heeded the rhetoric of Arab nationalism in its cause against Israel solidly backed the Arab oil embargo. As it continues to develop, Arab nationalism is increasingly running counter to Iranian national aspirations in the gulf. One of the best illustrations of the conflict is the dispute over the name of the gulf: the Iranians insist that it is the Persian Gulf and even take umbrage over the neutral term, "the gulf"; The Arabs have been just as insistent that it is the Arabian Gulf.

There are other factors influencing gulf politics. One, discussed in chapter 1, is the demographic differences of size, population, and attendant political-military power. Iran, Iraq, and Saudi Arabia are the "big powers" of the gulf. Of the three, Iran has the largest and best-equipped military establishment and is attempting to strengthen it even further through arms acquisitions, chiefly from the United States. To the extent that military force is effective in halting the spread of radicalism in the gulf, Iranian military power can play a stabilizing role. However, were Iran to use its military force on the Arab side of the gulf unilaterally and without adequate consultation among its conservative Arab neighbors, even against some radical threat, it could result in opposition rather than cooperation from the Arab states. Clearly, Iranian military power could be destabilizing as well as stabilizing, depending on how it is used.

In contrast to the Iranian armed forces—which, except for two rotating battalions which have seen duty in Oman, have had no combat experience—the Iraqi armed forces have had recent and relatively large-scale combat experience in the October 1973 Arab-Israeli war and at home in the Kurdish insurgency. At the same time, political purges and ethnic divisions have been an inhibiting factor in their effectiveness; many considered that the Iraqi army's actually getting to the front in the 1973 war was a major logistical accomplishment. Thus, in trying to evaluate the relative strengths of the Iraqi and Iranian armed forces, it is an open question as to whether either could successfully mount an offensive against the other, though both probably have the capability to defend their own territories. In terms of naval strength Iran appears to be more clearly preponderant.

Saudi Arabia, large and sparsely populated, has the smallest military capability of the "big three." It is, however, building up its military voice in the regional security of the gulf.

The smaller states of the gulf—Kuwait, Bahrain, Qatar, the seven UAE shaykhdoms, and Oman—have little political or military power and could scarcely resist political ultimatums from any of the three big gulf states. Nevertheless, the ideological and nationalistic confrontations in the gulf tend to balance each other in restraining any of the larger gulf powers from seeking to impose its will on the smaller states. For example, Iraqi aspirations in the gulf are checked by conservative Saudi Arabia and Iran, whereas Iranian national aspirations are restrained by Arab nationalist sentiments which are shared by the conservative Saudis and the radical Iraqis alike. The resulting political equilibrium allows the smaller gulf states some scope for independent political decision making, probably much more than they otherwise would have.

Among the smaller shaykhdoms, there is also a political dynamic. Prior to the discovery of oil, the shaykhdoms were all poor. Kuwait and Bahrain discovered oil first, and Kuwait's oil revenues caused it to develop more rapidly than the others, both econom- ically and politically. For example, Kuwait attained full indepen- dence in 1961, a decade before the others. The other shaykhdoms, remembering the not too distant past when all were poor, began to feel resentfully that Kuwait treated them as poor relations. Dis- covery of oil in the lower gulf has helped to change that attitude. Moreover, as soon as the British announced their intention to withdraw from the lower gulf, Kuwait embarked on a very successful policy of helpful cooperation which largely dispelled its earlier negative image.

There still remains a dynamic of rivalry and cooperation, based on dynastic, territorial, historical, and other factors. At risk of oversimplification, one might say there is a tendency for shaykh- doms to be at odds with their immediate neighbors and to have good relations with the next shaykhdom over. For example, Qatar has a tradition of poor relations with Abu Dhabi on one side and Bahrain on the other, the latter conflict having its origins in Bah- rain's historical claim to northern Qatar, site of the first al- Khalifah capital. Similarly, Dubai is an intense rival of Abu Dhabi and Sharjah; Sharjah of Dubai and Umm al-Qaywayn; and so on. At the same time, Abu Dhabi gets along well with Bahrain and Sharjah, and Sharjah with Ras al-Khaymah, with which it has close dynastic ties. This complex political pattern can be very important at times. For example, although the British tried very hard be- tween 1968 and 1971 to effect a federation of all nine shaykh- doms, in the end Bahrain and Qatar chose to go it alone, unable to reconcile their differences.

The economics of the gulf will be discussed in more detail in a later chapter. Some general statements can be made at this point, however, on the impact of economics on regional politics. First of all, the concentration of wealth in the gulf, almost entirely from oil income, is enormous. It is therefore within the capability of nearly every ruler to co-opt potential dissidents through lavish social welfare and economic development programs. The existence of great wealth also increases the propensity of a regime to focus inwardly in its development programs. To the extent that this is the case, external disputes can take on relatively less urgency, a stabilizing factor.

On the other hand, increased oil revenues, particularly since the quadrupling of oil prices in 1973, have tended to broaden the political horizons, particularly of the bigger gulf states, not only in the context of the gulf, but in the broader Middle East region and even beyond. To the extent that such new aspirations conflict, particularly in light of the quantum increase in military arms transfers to the area in recent years, the concentration of economic wealth in the gulf could be potentially destabilizing as well.

Oil resources are not evenly divided among the gulf states. Four of the UAE shaykhdoms—Ajman, Umm al-Qaywayn, Ras al-Khaymah, and Fujayrah—have none at all. Saudi Arabia, Kuwait, and Abu Dhabi are fabulously wealthy in terms of per capita income; they are expected to accumulate foreign exchange balances in the coming years far exceeding their capability to invest them in their domestic economies, at least at efficiencies considered even minimally productive in the West. Iran and Iraq also have large oil incomes—some believe that Iraq's reserves are far greater than are presently estimated. Both countries have a greater capacity for internal investment than do Saudi Arabia, Kuwait, and Abu Dhabi, particularly in economic development. Qatar, Dubai, Bahrain, and Oman are moderately endowed with oil, and in 1974 Sharjah came on stream as the third oil producer in the UAE. Prior to the precipitous oil price rises in 1973, Bahrain, with a large, articulate labor force and declining oil production, and Oman, struggling against the Dhufar rebels, were financially hard pressed in their efforts to maintain stability. With greatly increased revenues, the economic burdens of internal and regional security have been considerably reduced.

The distribution of wealth as a factor in gulf politics is more apparent than real. This is in large part because all of the gulf states have either direct oil revenues or access to them. The only countries with no oil revenues are the four UAE shaykhdoms, and Shaykh Zayd of Abu Dhabi, president of the UAE, has been very generous in distributing funds to these poorer areas for economic and social development.

Territorial disputes have long been a basic political fact of life in the gulf. Not only are there few permanent features in the desert terrain characteristic enough to permit a definitely described boundary line, but also the need for boundary lines did not exist in the region until the development of oil resources. Traditionally, tribal affiliation rather than geography was the main determinant of political allegiance. Unfortunately, tribes often gave their allegiance to more than one political power and changed sides as they saw fit. Moreover, tribes tend to be mobile, covering large areas in their nomadic wanderings and often locating in the vicinity of other tribes with different allegiances.

The degree to which tribal allegiances transcended line boundaries until the recent past is illustrated in St. John Philby's account of the December 1922 Uqayr Conference when an attempt was made by the British representative, Sir Percy Cox, to delimit the borders of Najd with Iraq and Kuwait. According to Philby, Ibn Saud of Najd

> was by no means enamored of the seemingly meaningless proposition of a fixed frontier in a featureless desert which never had accurately been surveyed, and whose tribes had for centuries roamed over it without let or hindrance in search of water or pasture.[1]

At the time of this writing, most of the territorial disputes in the gulf region have been settled or at least allowed to lie dormant. The British, prior to their departure in 1971, had worked hard to resolve as many of them as possible. The most heated dispute at the time consisted of Iran's claim over Bahrain. The Iranians, who had controlled Bahrain off and on over the centuries, claimed that they had never ceded sovereignty nor recognized the ruler of Bahrain as an independent chief of state.[2] In the interests of gulf stability, the shah announced early in 1969 that he would not use force to promote his claim and would defer to the wishes of the Bahraini people on the issue of sovereignty. The Iranian call for a plebiscite or referendum was seen largely as a face-saving device. This, however, was not acceptable to the ruler of Bahrain, who took the position that the sovereignty of the regime was a fact and therefore not something to be bestowed by means of a plebiscite. After lengthy deliberations among the Bahrainis, Iranians, and British, it was finally agreed to allow a United Nations commission to enter Bahrain in order to ascertain the consensus of the people. On May 2, 1970, it reported that an overwhelming majority of Bahrainis supported an independent Bahrain, thus paving the way for Iran to relinquish its claim.

A second territorial dispute which the British endeavored to settle involved three small islands in the lower gulf, the Greater and

Lesser Tunb Islands and Abu Musa. The Tunbs were administered by Ras al-Khaymah, and Abu Musa by Sharjah. All three islands were claimed by Iran, which having relinquished its claim to Bahrain, was all the more adamant to gain control over them. The Abu Musa claim was further complicated by an offshore oil concession dispute between Sharjah and neighboring Umm al-Qaywayn, involving an extension of Sharjah's territorial waters from three to twelve miles.[3] This extension effectively deprived Umm al-Qaywayn of any part of the oil which was discovered within twelve miles of Abu Musa. Iran warned that no Abu Musa oil should be produced until its claims were settled.

After months of negotiation, a complicated formula was worked out whereby Iran was to place garrisons under its flag on the Tunbs and Abu Musa; and Sharjah would continue to exercise administrative control over the some 200 (Arab) inhabitants of Abu Musa. Provisions were also made for Iranian financial aid to Sharjah. The aid was to be phased out if oil were produced off Abu Musa, and the revenues of the oil were to be divided between Iran and Sharjah. By the terms of the formula the Arabs did not formally relinquish sovereignty of the islands, but Iran fully expects to retain them.

The arrangement came into effect on November 30, 1971, the day before the British relinquished their protective status in the gulf. Ras al-Khaymah, however, never agreed to it, and when Iranian troops landed on the Tunbs they were met by small-arms fire from a Ras al-Khaymah police detachment. As a further consequence, Shaykh Sagr of Ras al-Khaymah at first refused to join the UAE, but after realizing he could get little Arab support for his cause, he finally joined in February 1972.

There was some bitterness in Sharjah when its ruler, Shaykh Khalid, signed the agreement with Iran. His kinsman Shaykh Sagr bin Sultan, who had been deposed as ruler of Sharjah in 1965, tried to exploit this feeling in an attempt in January 1972 to regain the throne. The coup failed, largely due to the dispatching of Abu Dhabi troops by Shaykh Zayd, but Khalid was killed. In retrospect, although the islands dispute has been resloved for the moment, Arab claims of the "Arab character" of the islands could always reopen the dispute.

On July 29, 1974, Prince Fahd of Saudi Arabia and Shaykh Rashid of Dubai, acting in his capacity as vice-president of the United Arab Emirates, initiated a preliminary agreement ending the long-standing Saudi-Abu Dhabi border dispute. Shaykh Zayd, as president of the UAE, did not initial the agreement for protocol reasons, but it was he who invited Fahd to Abu Dhabi.

At the center of the dispute historically was the al-Buraymi Oasis. Though claimed by the Saudis from the nineteenth century, the oasis had not been directly administered by them since 1871 when the then Saudi governor departed during a period of Saudi internal political strife. For the next sixty years, al-Buraymi, which consists of nine villages, lived in quasi-independence on the fringes of the political power of Abu Dhabi, Oman, and Saudi Arabia.

Another area in the dispute was al-Liwa (al-Jiwa), the collective name for a string of date palm oases in a line about sixty miles long from northwest to southeast, considerably west of al-Buraymi. Several tribes inhabit al-Liwa. Of these, the Manasir tribesmen in this area traditionally gave their allegiance to the Saudis, but the Bani Yas were loyal to Abu Dhabi, only about one hundred miles away and originally settled by Bani Yas from al-Liwa. In many cases, however, even the Bani Yas paid both traditional date crop and religious taxes (*zakat*) to the Saudis as well as to Abu Dhabi.

Between 1935 and 1937 the Saudis negotiated for a boundary settlement with Britain, which was the protecting power for Abu Dhabi and also Oman. The Saudis based their claim on their nineteenth century control and on continual tribal allegiance, including payment of taxes. The British countered that such allegiance and tax payments among nomadic tribes were too irregular to prove sovereignty and that sections of the tribes in question also paid allegiance and taxes to Abu Dhabi and Muscat. Moreover, no other form of Saudi authority had been exercised since 1871. At one point, the Saudis offered to give up their claim to Buraymi and al-Liwa for concessions further west, but negotiations failed. (Interestingly enough, the terms of the present agreement appear to approximate those offered in the mid-thirties by the Saudis.)

In 1951-52 Saudi-British talks were resumed but again reached a deadlock. By this time, oil discoveries in the area had considerably raised the stakes of a settlement for all concerned. In August 1952 the Saudis dispatched Turki bin 'Utayshan and some forty Saudis to al-Buraymi, where Turki assumed the title of amir or governor. In 1954-1955 Britain and Saudi Arabia submitted their cases to arbitration by a noted international jurist, Charles

De Visscher.[4] But by September 1955 the arbitration collapsed, and in October a British-led force drove out the Saudis and some 1,000 to 1,500 inhabitants of al-Buraymi, who went into exile in Saudi Arabia. The British then proceeded to defeat the imam of Oman who also fled to Saudi Arabia. From that point on, Oman and Abu Dhabi have shared the administration of the oasis.[5]

Subsequent efforts to settle the dispute failed, and counterclaims over an oil field in the disputed area (called Zararah by Abu Dhabi and Shaybah by the Saudis) further complicated matters. In recent years, pride was probably as great an obstacle as any other factor to reaching a settlement: Shaykh Zayd, before becoming the ruler of Abu Dhabi in 1965, was governor of al-Ayn, the principal Abu Dhabi town in al-Buraymi (and now the site of a Hilton hotel); King Faysal, on his part, wanted deference shown to the Saudis' historical position along with a tangible quid pro quo in return for giving up al-Buraymi. (Al-Liwa by this time was no longer disputed by Saudi Arabia.)

In the end both sides seem to have become reconciled. The Saudis have given up their claim to al-Buraymi. In return they have apparently received most of the Zararah/Shaybah oil field and a corridor between Abu Dhabi and Qatar to the Persian Gulf to pipe its Shaybah oil. The settlement of this long intractable dispute greatly enhances regional stability in that it removes a major source of friction between two conservative gulf states, enabling them to cooperate on a wide range of issues. There is every indication, however, that Zayd will continue to follow an independent course on oil and other policies when he deems it to be in Abu Dhabi's and the UAE's interests to do so.

Settling of the al-Buraymi dispute should also make it easier for Saudi Arabia and Oman to cooperate more closely. A separate Saudi-Omani border agreement is being negotiated at the time of this writing. Relations between Oman and Saudi Arabia, which had been very strained since 1955, thawed in December 1971 when King Faysal invited the new sultan, Qabus, to visit Riyadh. In May 1975 the Saudis, as a sign of good will, offered to assist and ease Oman's financial crisis. The amount of Saudi aid had been reported to be at least $100 million.

Nine months after the Saudi-Abu Dhabi border dispute was settled, a potentially even more explosive dispute was also resolved. At the March 1975 meeting of Opec in Algiers, President

Boumedienne announced that Iraq had agreed to the Shatt al-Arab River boundary with Iran in return for Iran's ending its support of the Kurdish insurgency in Iraq led by Mullah Mustafa Barzani. A formal agreement on land and sea borders and prohibition of border violations was signed by the foreign ministries of the two countries on June 12, 1975.

The Shatt al-Arab, which is formed by the confluence of the Tigris and Euphrates rivers in Iraq, forms the Iraqi-Iranian border in its lower reaches. According to an Ottoman-Persian treaty in 1847, reaffirmed by a protocol in 1913, the Ottomans owned the river to the highwater mark on the Persian side.[6] Modern Iraq fell heir to the Ottoman claim, but beginning in the 1930s Iran contested it. The present shah's father, Reza Shah, who had seized power in the 1920s, protested to the League of Nations, arguing that the center of the river (thalweg) should be the border.

A new treaty was drawn up in 1913 and extended in 1937. Iraq still retained possession of the river to the Iranian shore, but Iran was granted sovereignty out to the thalweg of those portions of the Shatt al-Arab adjacent to Abadan and Khorramshahr. It was the 1937 treaty which Iran unilaterally repudiated in February 1969, saying that Iraq had violated the treaty and, additionally, it was "contrary to all international practices and principles of International Law relating to frontiers."[7] Iraq retaliated by deporting a sizable number of Iranian Shi'a Muslims from Iraq. The dispute thereupon entered a period of more or less stalemate.

By 1974, Iranian-Iraqi relations had reached an all-time low, in large measure over Iran's support of the Kurdish insurgency. On several occasions Iraqi and Iranian troops actually exchanged fire in border areas. Evidently, however, neither side wished to pursue their confrontation to open hostilities, being more concerned with domestic and other foreign policy issues. Finally, in reaching a rapprochement in 1975, the long-standing Shatt al-Arab dispute was finally resolved.

There are still two territorial issues which have not been totally resolved. The Iraqi-Kuwaiti border dispute is one of them. Iraq has never formally relinquished its claim to Kuwait, a claim based on the territorial limits of the Ottoman Sanjak of Basrah. There was a period of tension when Kuwait obtained complete independence from the British in 1961 and Iraq briefly reasserted its claim. Over time the tension died down, but in March 1973 border tension reappeared as Iraq sought Kuwaiti territory in order to obtain greater territorial depth for the defense of the naval base it was developing at Umm Qasr. An armed clash occured on March 20, as Iraqis occupied a Kuwaiti police post on the border. The Iraqis subsequently withdrew, and although there was a brief border flurry in late 1974, they have not pressed their claims since in a hostile manner.

Iraq nevertheless appears determined ultimately to gain control over at least parts of the Kuwaiti islands of Bubayan and Warbah, which command the entrance to the estuary on which Umm Qasr is situated. Iraqis have hinted that they may attempt some sort of leasing arrangement. In terms of transfer of sovereignty, however, Kuwait could not give up the islands. It is not simply a question of national pride. Were Iraq to gain sovereignty over the islands, Kuwait would lose hundreds of square miles of offshore oil rights.

A second territorial question involves those parts of the gulf median line between Iran and the Arab side of the gulf which have not yet been agreed upon. The Saudi-Iranian median line had been hotly contested by both sides until an agreement was reached in 1968. Elsewhere in the gulf, there are large portions of the line still undrawn. Since billions of dollars of offshore oil could be at stake, a new discovery in the middle of the gulf could set off another median line dispute, threatening the stability of the area.

Another factor in gulf politics is the potential for political subversion. At one end of the spectrum of those who subscribe to political change are a host of covert political groups, some of which form and dissolve with great rapidity as internal disputes among their members wax and wane. At the other end are active insurgents such as those involved in the rebellion being waged until recently by the Kurds in Iraq, and those in Oman's southwestern Dhufar province.

Among the better-known subversive groups in the gulf is the Arab Nationalists movement (ANM). Founded at the American University of Beirut in 1948 by a group of young intellectuals, the ANM began as a small group of militant Marxist-socialists, including Palestinian fedayin leaders George Habbish, Naif Hawatama, and Ahmad Jabril. In 1968 the group began to split up, and by 1971 it had agreed to independent country-based organizations. Although their activities are theoretically co-ordinated by a higher executive committee, in fact each group is answerable only to itself. Thus, the ANM has evolved into more of a loose ideological brotherhood than a political organization.

The ANM has profoundly influenced radical groups in the gulf. In Kuwait it is overt and, under the leadership of Dr. Ahmad al-Khatib, has more or less eschewed violence in achieving its aims. There are, however, some more militant ANM members in Kuwait who take a different view. The radical National Front regime in South Yemen also had ANM antecedents, and the leadership of the Dhufar insurgency is associated with the ANM. Although all these organizations are independent, they do support each other's activities. Thus it was largely with PDRY support that the ANM rebels in Dhufar were so successful in the early 1970s.

The Ba'th party is also active in the gulf. Its members are divided into two wings, reflecting the Iraqi-Syrian Ba'th split. Each wing is supported by its Syrian or Iraqi patron and is in competition with the other. All, however, espouse the general Ba'thi goals of Arab unity, socialism, and antiimperialism.

The National Liberation Front of Bahrain is another fairly old sub-versive group, but unlike the ANM and Ba'th groups with outside ties, it is wholly indigenous to Bahrain. It is a Marxist organization with appeal among Bahraini intellectuals, one of the largest groups of intellectuals in the Arab shaykhdoms. Many of its leaders were exiled in the 1960s, but younger members appear to be maintaining the organization. They include Dr. Abd Al-Hadi Khalif, who was elected but not allowed to take his seat after the 1974 parliamentary elections.

The Palestinian fedayin groups are also represented in the gulf. Since their principal aim is to obtain money and political support from the gulf states and the relatively large resident Palestinian populations (e.g., over 200,000 in Kuwait alone), they are not, strictly speaking, subversive organizations in the same sense as the others. Nevertheless, there are ties between local subversive groups and the Palestinians, particularly among those with a common ANM background. George Habbash's Popular Front for the Liberation of Palestine, for example, has cooperated with the ANM in Kuwait, South Yemen's National Front regime, and the Dhufar rebels.

With the Iraqi-Iranian rapprochement in March 1975, the Kurdish rebellion has once again collapsed and its leader, Mullah Mustafa Barzani, lives in Tehran under house arrest. All the ingredients for a resumption of the insurgency are still there, however. The Kurds have always felt discriminated against by the Arab-dominated governments in Baghdad. They have periodically staged uprisings to demand a greater measure of local autonomy. The Baghdad government had agreed in March 1970 to extend more rights to the Kurds, but the agreement soon broke down and by 1974 a full-scale insurgency was in progress, supported by Iran.

Whether or not the Kurds remain subdued depends on several factors. One is the strength of the Iraqi regime; the more it can solidify its position, the less able will the Kurds be to revolt. Another is the amount of outside aid the Kurds can obtain. Iran had been the principal donor in recent years, but the availability of Iranian aid in the future will depend very much on the state of Iraqi-Iranian relations. Finally, there is the matter of Kurdish leadership. Barzani is aging and no other leader has his prestige. Though he has been given every political label from communist to conservative, Barzani is essentially a Kurdish nationalist. Depending on the political climate, if a new Kurdish leader emerges who espouses a radical litany, it could have political repercussions not only in Iraq, but in the gulf region as well.

The other insurgency in the gulf, the Dhufar rebellion, also seems to have stabilized in favor of the government.[8] It originally began as an irredentist movement appealing to the wild Qara and al-Kathiri tribesmen of Dhufar's Qara mountains who sought to oust the sultan, Said bin Taymur. The leaders of the movement were mainly Dhufaris who had found work in the post-World War II oil boom in the gulf and had come in contact with Marxist and radical Arab nationalist ideas. In 1964 the Dhufar branch of the ANM, the Dhufar Charitable Association (which had broken off from the ANM in 1962), and the Dhufar Soldiers' Organization, made up of Dhufari veterans of the army and police forces of the gulf shaykhdoms, all combined to form the Dhufar Liberation Front (DFL).

With the help of South Yemen, which became independent in November 1967, the ANM members of the DLF solidified their control of the organization. At the second party congress, held at

Harmin in central Dhufar in September 1968, the DLF adopted a program to increase the scope of their operations and changed its name to the Popular Front for the Liberation of the Occupied Arab Gulf (PFLOAG). In 1970 a similar group of radical anti-Sultan subversives from all over Oman banded together to form the National Democratic Front for the Liberation of Oman and the Arabian Gulf (NDFLOAG). This group merged with the Dhufar group in 1971, calling itself the Popular Front for the Liberation of Oman and the Arabian Gulf (also known as PFLOAG).

Operations in the north, undertaken by NDFLOAG, went poorly almost from the start, causing the movement to lose some of its sympathizers. In July 1970 Said bin Taymur was ousted and replaced by his son Qabus, enabling the government to concentrate on countermeasures. In Dhufar, however, PFLOAG was continuing to gain ground, successfully occupying most of the mountains surrounding the Dhufar plain. The rebel initiative reached its peak in July 1972 when over seventy insurgents were killed in a pitched battle with Omani troops at Marbat. By early 1974 PFLOAG was increasingly on the defensive. The quadrupling of oil prices in 1973 eased the financial burden, and the addition of Iranian combat troops in 1973 and 1974 and of Jordanian troops in early 1975 helped the government gain the initiative. Finally, in December 1976, the Oman government declared the insurgency to be over.

With government troops apparently establishing control in Dhufar, the insurgency seems to be entering a new phase. In January 1974 PFLOAG's name was shortened to the Popular Front for the Liberation of Oman (PFLO), reflecting a reduction in scope. Renewed emphasis was placed by the insurgents on political action in contrast to military action.

The Omani regime could be quite vulnerable to this change in strategy. It is devoting all the resources it can spare from the counterinsurgency program to developing its long-neglected economy. In any such attempt, corruption and inefficiencies are bound to crop up and development programs can easily get bogged down. In early 1975 Oman had so overextended its economy that it faced a severe cash liquidity crisis. The crisis could have had disastrous political effects had it not been for the May 1975 Saudi loan. On balance, however, Oman seems to have weathered the Dhufar crisis and its economic problems fairly well and appears again on the way to economic and social development.

The Foreign Policies of the Gulf States

One of the complicating factors in studying gulf politics is that the political relations among the states are influenced to a great degree by their interests beyond the immediate gulf area. Indeed, it has been only in the past few years that the big three—Iran, Iraq, and Saudi Arabia—began to look at the gulf as a separate area of policy interest and not merely a subcategory of Middle Eastern, Indian Ocean, or Arab and Muslim world politics. The change came with the 1968 British announcement of its decision to end its security status in the gulf and was intensified by the world focus on the gulf in the aftermath of the 1973-1974 energy crisis.

Iran's foreign policy horizons have expanded enormously over the past twenty years. In 1953 the ouster of Premier Mussadiq reestablished the authority of the shah. Initially, while the shah concentrated on consolidating his authority at home, his foreign policy horizons were largely bounded by attention to immediate external security threats to his regime. These threats were perceived to emanate primarily from the Soviet Union. To meet the Soviet threat, Iran in 1955 joined the Baghdad Pact, later known as the Central Treaty Organization or CENTO. In 1959 it concluded a bilateral defense treaty with the United States. (The United States also signed similar treaties with Pakistan and Turkey in lieu of joining CENTO.) The U.S.-Iranian treaty became the legal basis for subsequent U.S. military sales and training programs.

In the meantime, Iran set about to improve its relations with the Soviet Union. Between 1954 and 1958, the Soviet-Iranian border was demarcated. In 1962, after the shah stated that he would allow no foreign offensive missiles to be deployed on Iranian soil, Soviet-Iranian relations improved measurably. By the mid-1960s, Iran was the recipient of rather extensive Soviet aid, including the construction of Iran's first iron and steel mill at Isfahan. Additionally, Iran purchased military equipment from the Soviet Union, including trucks, armored personnel carriers, and antiaircraft guns. However, despite the shah's policy of improving relations with the Soviet Union, he remains staunchly anticommunist. He looks on his relations with the Soviets mainly as a means of avoiding tensions with a potentially overwhelming adversary and also as a means of asserting a more independent foreign policy between the communist and Western worlds.

By the mid-1960s, cold war tensions had begun to abate. In Iranian eyes, however, a new external threat to Iranian security was emerging in the form of militant Arab nationalism. Iran's cordial attitude toward Israel was a major thorn in the side of Iranian-Arab relations, particularly among the Arab militants, and in 1960 Egypt's President Nasser unilaterally broke diplomatic relations with Iran over its ties with Israel. Iraq, on January 23, 1970, expelled the Iranian ambassador over the Shatt al-Arab dispute, and in December 1971, in reaction to Iranian occupation of the Tunb Islands and Abu Musa, also completely broke relations with Iran.

Since then, Iran has initiated a cautious policy of rapproachement with the Arab radicals. Diplomatic relations with Egypt were restored on August 29, 1970, shortly before Nasser's death. In May 1974 the shah offered economic aid to Egypt and in January of the following year he paid a visit to Cairo. In Iran's eyes, the improved relations with Egypt were considerably enhanced by what it perceived to be a more moderate Egyptian stance than in the 1960s when Egypt was espousing the spread of militant Arab socialism.

In the aftermath of the October 1973 Arab-Israeli war, Iranian relations with the Arab states improved still more. Diplomatic relations were restored with Iraq, although tensions between the two countries remained high for another two years. The shah also publicly sided with the Arabs in calling for an Israeli withdrawal from lands occupied in the June 1967 Arab-Israeli war. With regard to the militant Arab states, Iran remains openly hostile only to PDRY. The hostility is most easily seen in the Dhufar insurgency in which PDRY is supporting the insurgents and Iran has provided combat troops in support of the sultan.

The British decision to withdraw from the gulf was seen by the shah as both a threat and an opportunity.[9] The threat of the British departure, as he saw it, was that the gulf would be deprived of a British security umbrella. Iran did not wish to see radicalism, whether militant Arab nationalism or Soviet- or Chinese-supported communism, spread into the area; nor did he wish to see another Western power such as the United States take over the British role.

The opportunity was that, probably for the first time, the shah felt politically secure and militarily powerful enough for Iran to achieve hegemony in the gulf, at least in a security sense. Since 1953 the shah had been building up his armed forces until they were the largest in the gulf. After 1968 he embarked on an even more ambitious military-development program commensurate with his concept of Iran's expanded security role. In the process, he had by 1975 negotiated for the purchase of over $9 billion worth of arms, mostly from the United States.

In sum, Iran's world view envisions a basic dichotomy between the powerful industrialized states of East and West and the weak states of the third world. While firmly tied to the free world economically and politically, Iran is determined to change its position from a weak third world state to a more powerful industrialized state, somewhat in the way that Japan has made the transition within the free world, and perhaps that China is in the process of doing in the communist world. For Iran, the key to that transition is oil. Therefore, more than any of the other OPEC members, Iran is politically committed to maximizing its oil revenues to the greatest possible extent. This goes far to explain why Iran has taken the leadership within OPEC for maintaining high prices but opposing the prorating of production cuts.

For all its militant ideology, *Iraq* has not really pursued an active foreign policy in recent years. Estranged from nearly all the Arab states, conservative and radical, and also from Iran, the Baghdad regime remained relatively isolated politically throughout the 1960s and early 1970s. Moreover, much of the attention of the regime was focused on the domestic problems.

The areas of policy interest receiving top priority were the Arab-Israeli war and financial and training support for subversive groups, particularly in the gulf. The Iraqi regime displayed a highly developed encirclement syndrome in which they saw themselves surrounded on every side by adversaries: Arab conservatives, Israel, Syrian Ba'thists, and Iran.

In seeking support against all their perceived enemies, the Iraqis turned primarily to the Soviet Union. Their good relations with the Soviets were further cemented by a Treaty of Cooperation and Friendship signed in 1973. The Soviets are also the major supplier of Iraqi military arms and equipment, and have supervised the construction and improvement of Iraq's naval base at Umm Qasr. Despite close Iraqi ties with the Soviet Union, however, it would be a mistake to conclude that Iraq is a Soviet client state or satellite. The Iraqis after a colonial past are highly sensitive to any perceived encroachment on their sovereignty, even by the Soviets.

Of all Iraqi foreign policy concerns, the Arab-Israeli problem probably looms largest. Iraqi troops fought in both the 1967 and 1973 Arab-Israeli wars; the government supports a Palestinian fedayin group, the Arab Liberation Front; and Iraqi policy has been consistently uncompromising against giving any concessions to Israel for the sake of a peace settlement.

Iraq has supported subversive groups since the 1958 revolution overthrew the monarchy, and the current Ba'thi regime, which came to power in 1968, is no exception. Many of the followers of the old imam of Oman, calling themselves the Oman Revolutionary movement (ORM), were trained in guerrilla tactics in Iraq. Dhufar rebels and other subversives received training and support from Iraq also. Some observers have speculated that with the collapse of the Kurdish insurgency Iraq would devote more resources to subversive activities in the gulf. Although its support of these groups is no doubt continuing, Iraq, at least for the moment, appears to be preoccupied with the Arab-Israeli dispute and internal development.

Since the October 1973 war Iraq has moved, albeit cautiously, away from its former political isolation. In part this has been motivated by the psychological victory the Arabs achieved in the October war, which restored the pride they had lost in the humiliating defeat of 1967 and enabled them to bury their differences for the sake of the common Arab cause. In addition, Iraq would like to invest its post-1973 oil revenues in more extensive domestic economic development. It has, therefore, moved to lessen tensions with its neighbors in order to concentrate more of its energies on internal development.

Saudi Arabia's foreign policy is, of all the gulf states, the most influenced by Islam, and the Saudi world view focuses foremost on the Islamic world. The Saudis follow the strict teachings of the Wahhabi revival. As keepers of Islam's two most holy places, Mecca and al-Madinah, they see themselves as protectors of the faith and the Islamic way of life.

The late King Faysal evolved a highly developed Islamic foreign policy. For him, the greatest threats to the Islamic way of life were atheism, which he saw alike in all radical doctrines from Marxism to Arab socialism, and Zionism, which he distinguished from religious Judaism as a political movement seeking to acquire sacred Arab soil. Faysal was particularly incensed at Israeli occupation in 1967 of old Jerusalem and the Aqsa Mosque, the third most holy site in Sunni (orthodox) Islam.[10] He stated publicly on several occasions that he wished to enter an Arab Jerusalem to pray at the Aqsa Mosque before he died. His wish was never granted.

The dual threat, which Faysal called the Zionist-Communist conspiracy, became the underlying theme in Saudi foreign policy. To oppose Arab socialist doctrines, the King tried to submerge Arab nationalism in a broader concept of Islamic world solidarity. The Saudi-funded Muslim World League and, after 1969, the Islamic Foreign Minister's Conferences and the Saudi-based Secretariat were used for this purpose. After the Israeli occupation of Arab territories in 1967, Faysal attempted to enlist the Islamic world not only against Arab socialism, but in support of the Arab cause against Israel as well.

Since World War II the Saudis have looked on the Western world and particularly the United States as the principal bulwark against communism. They therefore do not wish to see the West weakened economically or even politically. Unfortunately for Saudi Arabia, they also see the United States as the vital supporter of Israel, the other part of the Zionist-Communist threat. This in part explains the anomaly of the Saudis being the leaders of the 1973 Arab oil embargo and the single country in OPEC to desire lowered oil prices for the sake of the free world economy.

King Faysal was so preoccupied with Islamic world affairs and the Arab-Israeli problem that he tended to overlook politics in his own back yard, the gulf and the rest of the Arabian Peninsula. The only exception was his antipathy for the Marxist regime in PDRY. The Saudis have financed dissident South Yemen groups since PDRY's independence in 1967.

Under King Khalid and Crown Prince Fahd, more Saudi attention may be focused on the gulf. It was Fahd, at King Faysal's behest, who initialed an agreement ending the Saudi-Abu Dhabi border dispute. The new administration also shows signs of deemphasizing the Islamic coloration of King Faysal's foreign policy, though at the same time leaving the substance of that policy largely untouched.

Like Iran, the Saudis have also placed a high priority on developing their armed forces. After consolidating the Kingdom of Saudi Arabia in 1932, King Abd al-Aziz had virtually disbanded his tribally based army by World War II. In 1947 the United States established a military airfield at Dhahran with a training component for the fledgling Saudi air force. A small British training mission was established the same year to create a modern Saudi army. It was replaced by the U.S. Military Training Mission in 1952. Still, the Saudis, who knew all too well how armies overthrow monarchies, saw no need to build up a powerful military force. As a precaution, they organized, parallel to the army, a tribally based National Guard as an internal security force loyal to the regime.

When Faysal became king in 1964, the Yemeni civil war pitted Egyptian-backed republicans against Saudi-backed royalists. An Egyptian military force of some 60,000 in Yemen constituted a definite threat to Saudi Arabia. By 1965 Faysal felt that the creation of a credible military force was imperative for Saudi Arabia and asked U.S. aid in upgrading the Saudi military establishment. The perceived need for a modern army and air force was reinforced during the 1967 Arab-Israeli war. Faysal kept his troops at home, realizing that they were insufficiently trained to participate; but he also concluded that in another round of fighting he would not have that option. The need for a modern army and air force was even further reinforced in 1968 by the British decision to withdraw from the gulf. In the same year, an Iranian naval vessel seized a Saudi oil rig in the gulf. The incident was resolved, but Faysal saw the need for a naval force as well, not as a weapon to be used against Iran, but rather to ensure that Saudi Arabia have an independent voice in gulf security.

The early 1970s witnessed a growing Saudi perception of its security needs. The radical threat of South Yemen and Iraq to Saudi Arabia's greater role in the Arab-Israeli dispute have all influenced that perception.

For *Kuwait*, lacking the physical power of the big gulf states, the use of oil revenues has long been the principal tool of its foreign policy. As in its domestic programs, Kuwait sees as one of the major objectives of foreign policy neutralization of potential opposition through a systematic foreign assistance program. At risk of being simplistic, one might say that Kuwaiti foreign policy operates to a great extent on the assumption that no one will wish to or allow any one else to kill the golden goose.

The policy has worked remarkably well. For example, in the

aftermath of the June 1967 war, Kuwait, along with Saudi Arabia and Libya, became a major contributor to Jordan and Egypt, based on commitments made at the Khartoum Conference.[11] Significantly, when Jordan became somewhat of a pariah in the Arab world after crushing the Palestinian commando groups in Jordan in September 1970, Kuwait stopped its payments to Jordan. Payments, however, were resumed after the October 1973 war. Kuwait has also been very generous in its support of the Palestinians, both directly and by eliciting contributions for the Palestinian cause from the large Palestinian community in Kuwait.

Kuwait has also utilized such institutions as the Kuwait Development Fund for implementing its foreign aid programs. Prior to 1973 Kuwaiti foreign aid was concentrated mainly on the Arab states. Since the quantum jump in oil prices, however, Kuwait has expanded the scope of its foreign aid program to include non-Arab members of the third world as well.

The gulf amirates—*Bahrain, Qatar,* and the *UAE*—have been engaged in foreign policy making since their independence in 1971. All pursue conservative political policies and free market economic policies. For the most part, their external interests are limited to gulf politics; international trade, particularly in oil; and the Arab cause.

Bahrain and Dubai had built up a fairly extensive *entrepôt* trade long before independence. Bahrain's international airport, for example, is a crossroads of European-Far Eastern traffic. Dubai was noted as a free port and a center for illicit gold trade to Iran and the Indian subcontinent long before the discovery of oil, and is still a principal purchaser on the London gold market. Its "free trading" dhows (the traditional Arab sailing vessels, now largely equipped with powerful engines to outrun coast guard vessels) have dealt in many other forms of contraband as well.

All of these countries are oil producers, and as with the other gulf states, international oil policies are important to them. Bahrain, however, is not a member of OPEC, and although the UAE is, neither Dubai nor Sharjah, oil-producing members of the UAE, participate in OPEC. This means that for practical purposes Abu Dhabi is the only UAE shaykhdom actively engaged in OPEC affairs. Abu Dhabi is also the only amirate with such a sizable oil income that its foreign aid program has had a major impact. Unlike the aid programs of Kuwait and other gulf donors, however,

Abu Dhabi aid, which has been extended throughout the third world, has to date not been very well coordinated nor tied to specific projects; partially as a result of large aid expenditures, Abu Dhabi experienced in early 1975 a cash liquidity problem. This problem developed despite a 1974 income of over $5 billion.

Whether or not the emirates had given much thought to the Arab-Israeli problem before independence, they were not required to do anything about it so long as Britain managed their foreign affairs. One of the first acts each country took at independence was to join the Arab League. Consequently, when the October 1973 Arab-Israeli war broke out, each of them was swept up in the Arab cause. When King Faysal called for an Arab oil embargo on October 17, 1973, they all followed suit. In the future, therefore, the emirates will no longer be shielded from Arab world politics and the Arab-Israeli problem. This will become a major determinant in foreign policy on any issue which Arabism touches.

Since its emergence from British-protected isolationism in 1970, *Oman* has had two major foreign policy aims: to gather support against the Dhufar rebels while at the same time neutralizing their supporters, and to gain acceptance of the Omani regime, particularly in the Arab world.

The counterinsurgency program, as described earlier, has been going fairly well for the government. The deployment of Jordanian combat troops has helped to reduce Arab criticism of Iranians fighting on Arab soil. Both have helped greatly in the war effort, and have also helped to lower the British profile in Oman's armed forces.

Ending Oman's political isolation is a much more complex problem, and in the opinion of at least one senior Omani official, it is one of greater long-term priority. The Arab states, led by Saudi Arabia, nearly all supported Imam Ghalib, expelled from inner Oman in 1955 by a British-led force. Oman's political isolation was reinforced by Sultan Said bin Taymur, who had become virtually a recluse in Salalah in the latter part of his reign, and by the fact that he depended on the British to administer many of the key functions of government, particularly defense and national security.

From the time he came to power in 1970, Sultan Qabus has attempted to end Oman's long period of isolation. In December of

1971 he visited the Saudi capital of Riyadh in what was to be the first step of reconciliation with Saudi Arabia. A reflection of his success in gaining Arab acceptance was Oman's joining the Arab League on September 29, 1971. Less than two weeks later, Oman became the one hundred thirty-first member of the United Nations.

NOTES

[1]H. St. John B. Philby, *Arabia* (London: Ernest Benn, 1930), pp. 290-91.

[2]Majid Khadduri, ed., *Major Middle Eastern Problems in International Law* (Washington, D.C.: American Enterprise Institute, 1972), p. 104.

[3]*Ibid.*, p. 104.

[4]Both sides presented a memorial stating their case. See *Memorial of the Government of Saudi Arabia: Arbitration for the Settlement of the Territorial Dispute between Muscat and Abu Dhabi on the one side and Saudi Arabia on the other, A.H. 1374/A.D. 1955;* and *Arbitration Concerning Buraimi and the Common Frontier between Abu Dhabi and Saudi Arabia: Memorial submitted by the Government of the United Kingdom of Great Britain and Northern Ireland, 1955.*

[5]For a pro-British account of the dispute, see J.B. Kelly, *Eastern Arabian Frontiers* (New York and London: Praeger, 1964).

[6]See E. Lauterpacht, "River Boundaries: Legal Aspects of the Shatt al Arab Frontier," *International and Comparative Law Quarterly* 9 (1960): 208-236.

[7]Khadduri, *Major Middle Eastern Problems*, p. 91.

[8]For an excellent account of the Dhufar insurgency, see D.L. Price, *Oman: Insurgency and Development, Conflict Studies* 53 (London: The Institute for the Study of Conflict, January 1975). A book taking the radical point of view is Fred Halliday, *Arabia without Sultans* (London: Penguin, 1974).

[9]The following discussion is based in part on an earlier paper by the writer, "US Strategic Interests in the Persian Gulf: Problems and Policy Analysis," delivered at the National Security Affairs Conference of the National War College, Washington, D.C., July 14-15, 1975.

[10]Many Westerners incorrectly believe the principal Islamic holy site in Jersualem is the gilded Dome of the Rock. The Aqsa Mosque actually sits to the side of the Dome of the Rock and has a much less imposing silver dome.

4

The Gulf and International Politics

Although the gulf would probably receive relatively little attention today from the Western world were it not for oil and the revenues oil generates, external interest in the gulf actually predates the discovery of oil by over 400 years. In 1498, the Portuguese sea captain Vasco de Gama, having rounded the Cape of Good Hope, landed near "Calicut," India. Another Portuguese captain, Alfonso D'Albuquerque, was subsequently appointed viceroy of Portuguese India at Goa and set out to establish a great Portuguese empire in the East.[1] He won two major engagements in the Straits of Hormuz in 1505, and two years later subjugated Oman's Batinah Coast. In 1515 the Portuguese finally captured the key trading city of Hormuz after several attempts and concurrently extended their hold northward to Bahrain.

For nearly a century thereafter, the Portuguese maintained a virtual monopoly in European seaborne commerce with the gulf. By the beginning of the seventeenth century, however, their power had begun to decline. In 1622 Hormuz fell to a joint British-Persian force. Portugal's last two outposts on the Arabian shore, Muscat and Khasab in Oman, were lost in 1650.

Following the decline of Portuguese ascendancy, there ensued a period of rivalry between the British and the Dutch, both expanding their empires in the East. The Dutch were predominant in the gulf in the mid-seventeenth century. However, an English-Dutch treaty against France in 1688 had the effect of subordinating Dutch interests to those of the British.[2] The Dutch position in the gulf was eclipsed entirely by 1766 when the British consolidated their position in India.

The initial British interest in the gulf was commercial and was exercised through the British East India Company. Chartered in 1600, this company was amalgamated with two smaller rival companies in 1708 and became the principal instrument of British power in the gulf for the next 150 years.[3]

The eighteenth century witnessed the rise of French imperial aspirations in the Indian Ocean, rivaling those of the British there and in the gulf as well. The recall in 1754 of the governor of the French East India Company, Dupliex, ended France's ambitions for an Indian empire but did not drive them entirely out of the area. In October 1759 they attacked Bander Abbas and forced the East India Company to transfer its Persian Gulf "residency" to Bushire (Persia) in 1763. However, company factories were still maintained at Basrah and Bandar Abbas.

The French threat to British interests in the East reappeared with Napoleon's invasion of Egypt in 1798. In that year the East India Company, acting for the British crown, signed an agreement with the ruler of Oman. The agreement, the first British treaty with a gulf state, was designed to keep the French out of the gulf.[4] A treaty of alliance against the French was also concluded between the British and the shah of Persia in 1801. British interest in the gulf by that time, however, had shifted. Political turmoil in the area throughout much of the eighteenth century had resulted in a drastic decline in trade, causing the East India Company seriously to consider withdrawing altogether. At the same time, the gulf was gaining in strategic importance as a line of communication with the increasingly important Indian empire.

The French threat receded with their expulsion from Mauritius in 1810, but a new threat had already begun to appear in the form of Arab privateers. Encouraged by the teachings of the Wahhabi religious revival, Arab mariners, particularly from the Qawasim tribes of Ras al-Khaymah and Sharjah, attacked the merchant ships of unbelievers in the gulf and the Indian Ocean. Their activities earned for the lower gulf coast the epithet, "Pirate Coast." From the mariners' perspective, however, it was a religious duty to scourge the shipping lanes of unbelievers such as the British and non-Wahhabi Muslim "heretics."

Between 1805 and 1819, the British dispatched several expeditions to the gulf to quell the "pirates," but to no avail. Then, taking advantage of the defeat of the Saudis by Ibrahim Pasha in 1818 and the collapse of Wahhabi power in eastern Arabia, the British decided to crush the Qawasim privateers once and for all. They mustered a force of two men-of-war, nine cruisers, and 3,500 troops off Ras al-Khaymah in December 1819. On December 22 the Qasimi shaykh Hassin bin Ramah, whose descendants still rule in Ras al-Khaymah and Sharjah, surrendered.[5]

The result of the British victory was a treaty which became the cornerstone of the British political, strategic, and economic presence in the gulf for 150 years. Called the General Treaty for Suppressing Piracy and Slave Traffic, it was signed by the Qasimi shaykhs and their allies.[6] In addition, the shaykhs of Abu Dhabi and Bahrain, though not considered piratical by the British, were allowed to sign at their request.[7]

Although the 1820 treaty stopped Arab attacks on British shipping, it did not bring peace, for there was no provision banning the Arab shaykhdoms from making war on each other. In 1835 the official British resident obtained a truce according to which the shaykhdoms refrained from war on the seas during the six-month pearling season and the British refrained from interfering with wars on land. This truce, which was renewed each year, was so successful that in 1853 it was replaced by the Treaty of Maritime Peace in Perpetuity. This gave rise to the name, "Trucial Coast," in place of the earlier Pirate Coast.

Throughout the nineteenth century, British policies in the gulf and the Indian Ocean generally reflected their growing imperial interests. At the beginning of the century, the East India Company still administered British affairs in the gulf. In 1822, however, when Lt. John Macleod was appointed resident in the Persian gulf, his responsibility was protection of British imperial interests rather than of commercial interests. In 1858 the activities of the British East India Company were taken over entirely by the British government of India. Thenceforth, until Indian independence in 1947, British gulf affairs were the responsibility of the Indian government.

By the end of World War I, a series of interlocking treaty relationships were established with Qatar (1869, 1913, 1916) and Kuwait (1899). With Britain's position of major influence in Persia and the creation of the British-controlled Mandate in Iraq in 1920, these relationships made the gulf virtually a British preserve.

After World War II, the British position in the gulf waned rapidly. In the early 1950s Iran began to exert her independence from outside influences; the 1958 coup in Iraq ended Britain's security and political role there; and in 1961 Kuwait regained her complete independence from British protection. But in the nine Gulf shaykhdoms and Oman, the British military and political presence was still considered to be the major stabilizing force. On January 16, 1968, British Prime Minister Harold Wilson announced to the House of Commons:

> We have decided to accelerate the withdrawal of our forces from their stations in the Far East...by the end of 1971. We have also decided to withdraw our forces from the Persian Gulf by the same date.... On the Gulf, we have indicated to the Governments concerned that our basic interest in the prosperity of the area remains: and as I have said, the capability we shall be maintaining here will be available.[8]

The announcement came as a surprise to many, both in the gulf and beyond it. After 150 years, the British were relinquishing their security role. An era had ended. When the Conservative party came to power in Britain in June 1970, it considered reversing the decision, or at least postponing the 1971 deadline. It soon realized, however, that, with Iranian and Arab opinion firmly opposed to postponement, the psychological moment for a reversal had passed.

The period from 1968 to 1971, when the British actually relinquished their security role in the gulf, was one of transition. The British attempted to leave the shaykhdoms as politically strong as possible. In an effort to resolve the territorial disputes over the Tunbs and Abu Musa, discussed in the previous chapter, they used their good offices to negotiate with all parties. On the matter of al-Buraymi and the Abu Dhabi-Saudi border dispute, they were less successful.

The main concern of the British was that some of the non-oil-producing Trucial States were too poor and too small to be viable political entities. Because Britain had never colonized the shaykhdoms but had merely provided them a security umbrella, the shaykhdoms had neither been introduced to modern political institutions nor unified into a larger, more viable entity. To remedy this, the British persuaded the shaykhdoms to agree on March 30, 1968, to federate. However, subsequent efforts to turn intention into fact, led by Sir William Luce, a distinguished British colonial official, met with only partial success. Bahrain was not entirely accepted by the others because of Iran's claim to it. When the Iranian claim was settled, Bahrain demanded a legislature in which representation was based on population, since its population (then 200,000) was nearly as large as the others' combined. When this demand was refused, Bahrain decided to withdraw from the federation and so became independent in August 1971. Qatar, a rival of Bahrain, then followed suit and became independent in September. The federation, now reduced to the seven Trucial States—Abu Dhabi, Dubai, Sharjah, Ajman, Umm al-Qaywayn, Ras al-Khaymah, and Fujayrah—became fully independent on December 1, 1971. As it turned out, however, Ras al-Khaymah, piqued over having a secondary role in UAE affairs and at the Iranian occupation of the Tunb Islands, which it claimed, refused to join the federation until February 1972.

In retrospect, the British decision appears to have been wise but precipitous. Although probably taking it for granted that the British would leave some day, none of the shaykhdoms at the time had seriously focused on the desirability of independence. In fact, many of them privately expressed dismay over the suddenly imminent prospect of losing the protective shield that Britain had provided since 1820. Nevertheless, the die had been cast, and it probably did not matter greatly what timetable the British set for their withdrawal; the period of exclusive British influence in the shaykhdoms ended on January 16, 1968. Thereafter, each shaykh, and other gulf rulers also, set out to obtain the most advantageous arrangements for the coming independence.

The British announcement of its intention to end its treaty obligations and withdraw its troops from the gulf caused foreign offices throughout the world to reevaluate their interests and policies toward the gulf. The quadruple oil price rise and the Arab oil embargo of 1973 and 1974 further focused world attention on the gulf. As a reflection of this new focus, nearly anyone, it seemed, who could name if not spell the Trucial States before 1968 was considered an "old gulf hand," and his expertise was in high demand.

The following is a brief synopsis of the leading world powers' interests in and policies toward the gulf, excluding the United States, which will be treated separately in a subsequent chapter. Economic and commercial relations, though mentioned briefly below, will be discussed more fully in the chapter on the economics of the gulf.

Britain

With the independence of India and Pakistan in 1947, Britain no longer needed to play a security role in the gulf to protect the imperial lines of communication to the East. At the same time, however, a new imperative for gulf security had arisen: oil. Not only was Britain dependent to a great degree on the gulf's oil for its own energy needs, but British Petroleum (BP), a corporate descendant of the Anglo-Persian Oil Company, was a primary producer in the gulf and one of the so-called "Seven Sisters," the seven major oil companies in the world.

By 1968 the Labour Party, then in power, had concluded that Britain's oil and commercial interests would not be appreciably threatened by the British withdrawal. Recalling the difficulties surrounding the British withdrawal from Aden in 1967, and the creation of a radical regime there, the Labour party concluded that it was better to leave before being asked than to wait for a radical nationalist movement to develop in the shaykhdoms.[9]

Current British interests in the gulf, then, can be said to focus primarily on oil and commerce. Exploiting the growing oil revenue market, including both the ambitious development plans of the area states and the long-standing commercial alliances developed during the period of British protection, British economic ties with the gulf are extensive. Much of the public- and private-sector British activity in the area, therefore, is engaged in protection and extension of those interests.

In the field of security, the withdrawal of the British protective status did not automatically mean the end of a British presence. Troops were withdrawn from the former British base at Sharjah, but the British still maintain base rights on the Omani island of Masirah.

In the gulf shaykhdoms, British military and security officers have stayed on after independence, either seconded from their British services or on direct contract to their host governments. Since the major threat to the stability of the area at present appears to be from internal subversion, the role of these British officers is very important to the security of the lower gulf.

In the long run, however, the British security role in the lower gulf cannot help but diminish. A number of the British advisors and other personnel resident in the gulf have been there for many years, and while their influence is great, it is also highly personalized. As these men retire or are replaced, their successors will not have the same degree of personal rapport with the gulf leaders, which can only be developed over a long period of time. Additionally, a number of the gulf leaders are finding it increasingly expeditious for political reasons to lower the British profile in governmental advisory positions.

In Oman, the British continue to play a large and direct role in security affairs. In addition to their Royal Air Force installation on Masirah, the Sultan's Armed Forces are still largely under British operational command. The counterinsurgency effort in Dhufar, for example, is directed by British officers under a British brigadier. Even in Oman, however, a major effort is under way to Omanize the armed forces, both the officer corps and the enlisted men, and the British are cooperating with the movement to lessen their military and security role there. Not only does a high British profile in the Omani armed forces present a political liability to Oman, but to Britain as well. One of the handicaps of the British operating in Dhufar is the fear that a high British casualty rate would be very unpopular at home and could result in Whitehall drastically reducing its military support to Oman at a time when that support is still sorely needed.

In sum, the British interests in the gulf are primarily commercial and economic. The British do retain a major security role as well, but this role will probably diminish over time.

France

Despite continuing interest in the Middle East and the Indian Ocean, France after the Napoleonic period never again challenged British imperial supremacy in the gulf. In the post-World War II period, the French came to rely increasingly on gulf oil. But the long, bitter Algerian revolution and France's cordial relations with Israel precluded any real French position of influence in the region, at least on the Arab side of the gulf. To offset its negative relations with the Arabs, France concentrated on Iran as the principal object of its economic and political policies in the gulf. Iran became the recipient of considerable French economic and technical assistance.

The resolution of the Algerian war in 1962 enabled France to seek stronger relations with the Arab world in general, and under President de Gaulle, the French began to exercise around the world a foreign policy increasingly independent from its Western allies. In the gulf area, France concluded a number of economic, commercial, and cultural agreements to strengthen its new relationship.

Despite the political overtones of French policy under de Gaulle and his successors, French interest in the gulf has been primarily economic and commercial. Even the military sales programs, notably to Iran and Abu Dhabi, which purchased a squadron of Mirage fighters using Pakistan as an intermediary, have a decided commercial cast. The main French military presence in the Indian Ocean is located at Djibouti, the capital of former French Somaliland and now the French-controlled Territory of the Afars and Issas.

The economic importance of the gulf to France, as to the rest of the industrialized world, stems from oil. More than other industrialized countries, however, the French have attempted to secure oil supplies through a policy which emphasizes their good relations with the area states, their increasing disassociation with pro-Zionist politics, and their independent policy as an alternative to alliance with either the United States or the Soviet Union.

Commercially, France seeks to increase exports to the area, in particular to offset the foreign exchange drain caused by the high price of oil. The French have had some successes, such as in the sale of communications equipment to Saudi Arabia, but in the main, military sales have been among their leading exports.

West Germany

In the latter part of the nineteenth century, Germany attempted to challenge British supremacy in the gulf. Kaiser Wilhelm II's policy of *Drang nach Osten* included a "Berlin to Baghdad" railroad project, for which Germany received a concession from the Ottomans in 1902. By extending the railroad to Basrah, the Germans envisioned that they could challenge British supremacy in the gulf. But after British protests to the Ottoman government, an Ottoman-German-British agreement was worked out in 1914 protecting Britain's position in the gulf.

World War I ended all German imperial aspirations in the gulf. There was a brief pro-Nazi movement against Britain in Iraq under Rashid Ali al-Qilani during World War II, but the movement was as much Arab nationalist and anti-British as it was pro-German. It was the pro-German sentiments of the shah's father, Reza Shah, which led the British and Russians to force his ouster in 1941.

Current West German relations in the gulf are largely economic and center around oil. Germany's strong economy has put it in an excellent competitive position in the area. But politically, German relations have been slow in obtaining a foothold. After World War II, relations were restored with Iran. However, Germany's policy of giving reparations to Israel made relations somewhat strained with the Arab states, and when Germany extended full diplomatic relations to Israel in 1965, the Arab states retaliated by breaking diplomatic relations with Germany. Additionally, until it was discontinued in 1969, the Hallstein Doctrine—which in effect forced states to choose between recognizing either East or West Germany—was another deterrent to good relations. In the last few years, however, German relations with the Arabs have improved, and West Germany has diplomatic representation throughout the gulf.

Japan

Of all the industrialized countries, Japan is the most dependent on gulf oil, which accounts for over 80 percent of its total imports. Thus, the politics of oil dictate Japan's policy toward the gulf to an even greater extent than is the case for most other countries. By the same token, the gulf is a primary target for Japanese exports, from automobiles to textiles. The importance of Japan's dependence on gulf oil was underscored by its decision in November 1973 to back off politically from Israel in order to be subject no longer to the Arab oil boycott. This decision was taken despite heavy pressure from its principal ally and trading partner, the United States.

The Soviet Union

Like the British and other West European powers, the Russians have also been interested in the gulf area for centuries. Unlike those countries, however, its interest has centered to a great degree on the direct political and military threats to the Russian heartland posed by various Muslim states on Russia's southern periphery, threats that were supported from time to time by various European powers.

By the nineteenth century, tsarist Russia had defeated the Tatars of the lower Volga and was expanding southward at the expense of Ottoman Turkey and Persia. Farther East, Russian expansion began to arouse fears in British India, setting the stage for a classical confrontation of imperial interests. Russian policies regarding its "southern tier" were essentially defensive in nature, seeking to establish a buffer area of weak Muslim states within the aegis of Russian political influence. There was also an element within the Russian leadership that sought to expand even farther southward, ultimately trying to establish a "warm water port" in the gulf as an outlet for growing Russian imperial and commercial interests. For a variety of external and internal reasons, the Russian Middle East imperialists were never wholly successful in achieving their aims.

For a time, Soviet Russia paid little attention to the gulf, or the Middle East in general, being preoccupied with foreign and domestic problems elsewhere. During World War II, however, the Soviets renewed their historical interest in the area. In 1941 the Allies decided to supply the Russian front through Iran. With the British occupying southern Iran, Russian troops moved into northern Iran where they remained throughout the war. Thus, in 1946 they were able to attempt the creation of puppet states in Iranian Azerbaijan and Kurdistan, albeit attempts that failed.

Post-World War II strategy in the gulf area reflected a mixture of the traditional defensive desire to create a buffer zone between the Russian heartland and hostile powers beyond, and a newer ideological desire to export communist revolution. The perceived threat in the former context came chiefly from the United States, which was seeking to create an alliance system through the Baghdad Pact and later CENTO to control Soviet policy aims. The target in the ideological context was the "masses" of Middle Eastern peoples "under the yoke of Western imperialist-dominated dictatorships."

Throughout the 1950s and early 1960s, Soviet strategy in the gulf was largely conceived in military terms. The attempt to carve out Azerbaijan and Kurdistan reflect that point of view. By the late 1960s, however, the Soviets appeared to be developing a more sophisticated and predominantly political strategy. This did not necessarily mean that the Soviets were changing their ideological stripes, nor that they would eschew the use of military force if force were deemed useful to them. It was rather that West and East had reached a nuclear stalemate which not only lessened the external conventional military threat to the Soviets but also called for different strategies to further the Soviet aims of expanding its influence.

The current Soviet strategy in the gulf is aimed at seeking to increase its political and economic influence in the area at the expense of the West and particularly the United States. In the case of Iraq and PDRY, the Soviets have expended a great deal of effort in buttressing relations. The armed forces of both countries are equipped largely with Soviet arms, and extensive technical aid and assistance has also been made available. The cornerstone of Soviet-Iraqi relations is a Treaty of Friendship which was signed in 1972.

The Soviets have also supported subversive movements in the gulf, both directly and through Iraq and PDRY. For example, the Soviet Union is the principal arms supplier for the Dhufar rebels (PFLO).

These activities would suggest a continuing militant and active Soviet posture in the gulf. Such is not necessarily the case, however, for the Soviets frequently find that their interests and objectives in the area are in conflict. The chief constraint to militant Soviet policy in the gulf is Soviet relations with Iran. The Soviets attempted to use the carrot rather than the stick in their efforts to wean Iran away from its close military and political relationship with the United States. Any overt Soviet military activity elsewhere in the gulf, either directly or indirectly through Iraq or PDRY, would almost certainly drive Iran even closer to a U.S. security orbit, which the Soviets do not see in their interests.

With this conflict of interest in mind, the Soviets have attempted to establish and maintain good relations with the conservative gulf regimes,[10] while supporting radical allies and covertly supporting national liberation movements in the area. In the main, the strategy has been passive rather than active in that it seeks to exploit targets of opportunity rather than attempting to create them by fomenting political unrest or military confrontations.

There is, however, a military aspect of Soviet policy toward the gulf. For the most part, its naval force in the Indian Ocean, exceeding in capability that of the United States, is used in the context of its overall political strategy—e.g., showing the Soviet flag, with all the psychological ramifications that it implies. At the same time, from the Soviet point of view, the northern reaches of the Indian Ocean, including the gulf, comprise one of the few areas where a deterrent naval force could be deployed with the capability to strike at the heart of the Soviet Union. Thus, the Soviets are very sensitive to the *potential* U.S. strategic threat from this area. In a more operational context, the Soviets seek access to shore facilities in order to extend, if ever necessary, the deployment duration of their own ships. It was in part with this in mind that they assisted in constructing Iraq's naval base at Umm Qasr.

Oil is also a major factor in Soviet interests in the gulf. The great dilemma facing Kremlin strategists, however, is what to do about it. On the one hand, it is quite obvious to the Soviets how dependent its free world adversaries are on gulf oil, militarily as well as economically. It would be tempting for the Soviet Union to think in terms of encouraging a more militant and punitive oil policy by the gulf producers toward the Western consumers. In this context, the Western oil companies have long been a major target of Soviet propagandists.

On the other hand, the Soviets may foresee the day when they themselves will be net importers of oil, and all present indications are that production to meet future Soviet demand will have to come largely from the gulf. In the interim period, oil is still one of the major foreign exchange earners for the Soviet Union. Thus, its own energy policies could quite possibly make it a competitor with gulf producers for free world markets. Such a situation could well conflict with Soviet political aims in the gulf.

There is another, though perhaps less crucial, constraint on the Soviets in attempting to interfere with oil shipments to the West. Any effort to interdict oil tankers moving through the Strait of Hormuz, which the shah fears may occur, would violate laws of the sea regarding international straits. Since the Soviets themselves are dependent on both the Bosporus and the Dardanelles in the south and the Baltic Straits in the north, they have traditionally taken a position supporting the right of passage through international straits.

In sum, the Soviet Union is confronted with a number of conflicting interests and policy aims in the gulf. In recent years these have tended to rule out the type of aggressive destabilizing policies witnessed at the height of the cold war.

Other Communist States

Compared to the Soviet Union other communist states have had a relatively small interest in the Persian Gulf. Even China, which would appear to have every reason to pursue an active gulf policy has in fact not done so. In the early 1960s China established commercial ties with Kuwait, and in 1966 it set up an office of the New China News Agency there. On March 21, 1971, Kuwait announced its decision to establish full diplomatic relations with China. Iran, after first expressing reservations about the growing communist presence in the gulf, followed suit on August 17.

Chinese diplomacy, essentially designed to oppose both Soviet and Western influence where Chinese interests are at stake, has not been very active. After 1967, the Chinese took over the leading role in training the Dhufar rebels, but by the summer of 1973 they had withdrawn. During a visit to Tehran in June 1973, the Chinese foreign minister, Chi Peng-Pei, implied that China would no longer participate in national liberation movements in the gulf.

In addition to China, Cuba and East Germany have had military and security training missions in PDRY. Beyond that, there has been little other communist activity in the gulf or its periphery.

Other States

There are a number of Arab and South Asian countries that have special political, economic, and security interests in the gulf. Jordan plays an important security role in several countries. In addition to the combat batallion it sent to Oman in early 1975, Jordan provides engineering and training support for Oman's army. It also provided a number of military officers attached to the Saudi National Guard, and has security officers in several of the gulf shaykhdoms. Isolated in the Arab world after he crushed the Palestinian fedayin organizations in Jordan in 1970, King Husayn sought political as well as economic support from the gulf states in return for military training and security assistance. At first these states were slow to accept Jordanian overtures. But with the new wave of Arab solidarity and rising oil revenues after the October 1973 war and oil price rises, Jordanian relations in the gulf region, particularly with the Arab states, have warmed considerably.

Pakistan and India also have interests in the gulf. The Indian subcontinent was traditionally a major trading center for gulf maritime trade, and continues to be so for the dhows that sail from Dubai, Oman, and elsewhere. It is also a major source of manpower for the rapidly developing oil shaykhdoms.

In the field of security, Pakistan has had a rather large military mission in Saudi Arabia, to which it is linked through common faith in Islam. Saudi midshipmen have also trained at the Pakistani naval academy. In Abu Dhabi, the Mirage jet fighters are flown by Pakistani pilots. There is also a Pakistani military mission in Oman. The Omani navy, under British command, has traditionally had Indian naval officers. More recently, however, these have been replaced by Pakistanis, in part due to the urging of the shah, who feared Soviet influence in India. In addition, many of the Omani troops are Baluchis recruited by the British in Pakistan.

India, which has national aspirations in the Indian Ocean area as a whole and has wished to counter Pakistani influence in the gulf, has also attempted to establish closer relations with the area states. The Indians have sent a small mission to supply training and advisors to the Iraqi air force, but Pakistan has sent military advisors to Iraq as well. A potentially destabilizing factor could arise if Iran's expanding political ambitions were to conflict with India's in the greater Indian Ocean area. Such a confrontation could have a great impact on gulf politics.

In sum, many states in the industrialized world, the communist world, and the third world have strong, often conflicting interests in the gulf. Some interests have developed over the centuries, others arose because of the gulf's commanding position as an oil producer. In looking at U. S. interests in the gulf, the rapidly changing configuration of these other interests must be taken into account.

NOTES

[1]R.B. Serjeant, *The Portuguese Off the South Arabian Coast* (Oxford: The Clarendon Press, 1963), p. 15. For a historical account of this period, see also Arnold T. Wilson, *The Persian Gulf: An Historical Sketch from the Earliest Times to the Beginning of the Twentieth Century* (London: George Allen and Unwin, 1954).

[2]See A.T. Mahan, *The Influence of Sea Power upon History, 1660-1785* (London: Methuen, 1965), p. 68.

[3]Wilson, *The Persian Gulf*, p. 70.

[4]"East India Company's Agreement with Imam of Musqat for Excluding the French from his Territories—12 October 1798," in J.C. Hurewitz, *Diplomacy in the Near and Middle East, A Documentary Record: 1535-1914,* 2 vols (Princeton: D. Van Nostrand Company, 1956), vol. 1, pp. 64-65.

[5]J.G. Lorimer, *Gazetteer of the Persian Gulf, Oman, and Central Arabia,* 4 vols (Calcutta: Superintendent of Government Printing, 1915), vol. 1, pp. 658-70. The operation also had the support of Oman.

[6]The text of this and other relevant treaties are found in C.U. Aitchison, *A Collection of Treaties, Engagements and Sanads Relating to India and Neighboring Countries.*

[7]A comparison of the signatories to the treaty and the present UAE shaykhdoms presents an interesting reflection of the politics of the area. Sharjah and Ras al-Khaymah were then under joint rule. Two of the signatories, Khatt-Fulaiyah and Jazirat al-Hamra, are now incorporated into Ras al-Khaymah, whereas present-day Fujayrah has been independent only since 1952. Kalba, a dependency of Shayjah on the Gulf of Oman, was also independent from 1936 to 1951. Dubai, though signatory, was a dependency of Abu Dhabi until 1833.

[8]Great Britain, Parliament, *Parliamentary Debates* London: Her Majesty's Stationery Office, January 16, 1968), vol. 756, cols. 1580-81.

[9]The public rationale for the withdrawal decision, emanating from defense studies begun in 1966, was economic. A defense estimate published simultaneously with the message to Parliament concluded that reductions in expenditure were necessary for balance of payments reasons, and that a reduction in commitments abroad must be made concomitantly with the reduction of military capability resulting from reduced expenditures. See Great Britain, Secretary of State for Defense, *Statement on the Defense Estimates 1968* London: Her Majesty's Stationery Office, 1967). In fact, the conditions

surrounding the decision appeared to have as much to do with domestic British politics as with either economics or foreign policy.

10Thus far, the Soviets have not been successful in establishing diplomatic relations with Saudi Arabia, Bahrain, Qatar, the UAE, or Oman.

5

Gulf Oil and Its Implications

If the beginning of any great historical period can be dated precisely, the modern oil era in the gulf began on May 28, 1901. On that day, Alfred M. Marriot signed an agreement on behalf of an Australian financier, William Knox D'Arcy, whereby Shah Mazafaar ed-Din of Persia granted D'Arcy the first Middle Eastern oil concession.[1] The concession included all of Persia except the five northern provinces adjacent to Russia. In January 1908, oil was discovered. Three months later, D'Arcy's interests were reorganized into the Anglo-Persian Oil Company (APOC).

The strategic importance of oil came to be recognized six years later. When Winston Churchill became first lord of the admiralty in 1911, the Royal Navy was already converting from coal to oil to power its ships, yet nowhere in the British Empire was there any supply of oil. On June 14, 1914, just two months before World War I, Churchill successfully passed through Parliament a bill to purchase a controlling 51 percent interest in APOC. The company's name was changed to the Anglo-Iranian Oil Company (AIOC) after Reza Shah adopted Iran as the new name of his country in 1935.

In May 1951 the nationalist prime minister of Iran, Muhammad Mussadiq, nationalized AIOC's concessions. Soon thereafter, lacking skilled manpower and marketing facilities, which were in the hands of the oil companies, Iran's oil production ceased and its customers went elsewhere. Without government revenues, Mussadiq's popularity began to wane. His attempt in 1953 to take complete control from the shah failed when a popular uprising swept him from office, reportedly with a boost from the CIA. The shah regained power and has maintained it ever since.

On October 24, 1954, a new agreement was signed with the oil companies. Iran was to keep the ownership of its oil through the National Iranian Oil Company (NIOC). But a consortium of international oil companies was created to handle production and refining operations. Members included AIOC, which has changed its name to British Petroleum (BP), 40 percent; Royal Dutch-Shell, 14 percent; Gulf, Exxon, Texaco, Mobil and Socal, each with 7 percent; Compagnie Francaise des Petroles (CFP), 6 percent; and a number of independent American oil companies collectively called the Iricon Group, 5 percent.

In Iraq, the development of oil concessions was vastly more complex, involving intricate diplomatic and commercial maneuvers, the details of which may never be known entirely. The initial entrepreneur was an Armenian from Constantinople, Calouste Sarkis Gulbenkian. Prior to World War I, Gulbenkian interested the Anglo-Saxon Petroleum Company (the precursor of the Royal Dutch-Shell group) in exploring for oil in Iraq, then called Mesopotamia and under the control of the Ottoman Empire. The prospects appeared good. Since ancient times, "everlasting sacred fires" fueled by escaping natural gas had burned near Kirkuk; and oil seeping through rocks in that area had been used in lamps for miles around. In 1911 Gulbenkian organized African and Eastern Concessions. Deutsche Bank, which had owned oil rights in conjunction with the Anatolia Railway Company (a part of the Berlin-to-Baghdad scheme), obtained an equity in the company, and in 1912 African and Eastern Concessions became the Turkish Petroleum Company (TPC).

In 1914 Gulbenkian drew up an agreement among British, German and Dutch interests which gave APOC a 50 percent share of TPC and both Deutsche Bank and Royal Dutch-Shell a 25 percent interest. Called the Red Line Agreement, it also eliminated competition among the TPC owners in developing Middle Eastern oil resources. For his part, Gulbenkian received a 5 percent beneficiary, nonvoting interest in TPC.[2]

After World War I, France received the 25 percent equity formerly owned by the Germans. The Compagnie Française des Pétroles (CFP) was formed to acquire these shares, and subsequently the French government acquired a 35 percent interest in CFP. In return for its equity, the French agreed, among other things, to support the British demands that the Musul oil fields be included in the new British Mandate of Iraq rather than in Turkey and that Iraq honor the TPC concession. The arrangement was confirmed in the San Remo Agreement of April 1920 and the Treaty of Sèvres in August 1920. With the establishment of Iraq as a British mandate, the Turkish Petroleum Company's name was changed to the Iraq Petroleum Company (IPC).

U.S. oil companies objected to the closed-door provisions of the Red Line Agreement. After the war, seven of them—Standard of New Jersey (now Exxon), Standard of New York (now Mobil), Gulf Oil Corporation, Texas Oil Company (Texaco), Sinclair, Atlantic Oil Company (now part of Atlantic Richfield or Arco), and Pan American Petroleum (Standard of Indiana)—created a joint venture known as the Near East Development Corporation. With the aid of the U.S. Department of State, they pressed for participation in IPC. In 1928 IPC equity was redivided, giving the American group (Sinclair and Texaco had dropped out) 23.75 percent equity in IPC. The British, French, and Dutch interests received an equal amount. As a condition for their share, the Americans accepted the terms of the Red Line Agreement, eschewing independent oil exploration in the Middle East. By World War II, IPC had achieved a near monopoly over exploitation of Iraqi oil.

Bahrain was the next site of an important oil discovery. Major Frank Holmes, a New Zealand entrepreneur and adventurer, went to Bahrain in the early 1920s to study its water resources. He seems to have been far more interested in oil, however, for he soon crossed over to what is now Saudi Arabia. With the help of Ameen Rihani, a Lebanese-American who was a confidant of King Abd al-Aziz, Holmes was awarded a Saudi oil concession in 1923. Holmes's company, Eastern and General Syndicate, only hoped to sell this concession. At first Gulf was interested, until it learned that it was prohibited from independent exploration by the terms of the Red Line Agreement. Holmes then sold the concession to Standard of California (Socal) in 1928. Socal was not a party to the Red Line Agreement, but Bahrain was under British protection, and oil exploration was limited to British Empire companies. To meet this requirement, Socal merely created a wholly owned subsidiary in Canada, the Bahrain Petroleum Company (Bapco). In 1932 Bapco discovered oil.

Socal also inherited Holmes's Arabian concession, which had lapsed. With the aid of the British explorer and writer H. St. John B. Philby and an American who had previously studied Saudi mineral resources, Karl Twitchell, Socal was able to obtain a new concession agreement from King Abd al-Aziz in 1933. The concession was assigned to a wholly owned subsidiary, the California Arabian Standard Oil Company (Casoc). It first discovered oil in 1935, but it was not until the seventh well was spudded in on March 5, 1938, that Saudi Arabia started on its way to becoming the world's greatest oil country. The first commercial quantities of Saudi crude were not produced until after World War II. On January 31, 1944, Casoc's name was changed to the Arabian American Oil Company (Aramco).

Socal had excess oil for its marketing facilities whereas the situation was just the opposite for Texaco. In 1935 the two companies combined their overseas interests in the Near East and Asia, placing control of Bapco and Aramco (then Casoc) under a jointly owned subsidiary, Caltex. In 1948 Standard of New Jersey (Exxon) and Standard of New York (Mobil) also bought into Aramco, after having first been obliged to modify their commitments to the Red Line Agreement.

Major Holmes was also interested in a Kuwaiti concession. He obtained the backing of Gulf Oil, for Kuwait was excluded from the Red Line Agreement. The British, however, also having a protective role over Kuwait, insisted that no non-British company be granted a concession. After several years of maneuvering, involving the U.S. State Department and British Colonial Office, the ruler of Kuwait granted a concession to the Kuwait Oil Company (KOC) in December 1934. It was owned jointly by Gulf and APOC (now PB). Even though oil was discovered in 1938, commercial production did not begin until after World War II. Subsequently, two smaller concessions were granted, but they have not produced any oil: Royal Dutch-Shell's Kuwait Shell Petroleum has a concession offshore, and the Kuwait-Spanish Petroleum Company, owned jointly by the Kuwait National Oil Company and Hispanoil, have an onshore oil concession.

Two other companies obtained onshore concessions in the former Neutral Zone between Kuwait and Saudi Arabia. In June 1948 the American Independent Oil Company (Aminoil) obtained a concession covering Kuwait interests in the zone, and in February 1949 the Getty Oil Company obtained a concession covering Saudi Arabian interests. A third company, the Arabian Oil

Company (Japan), obtained a concession from Saudi Arabia in 1957 and Kuwait in 1958 for oil rights offshore from the Neutral Zone. It began oil production in 1960.

Although the Neutral Zone later was dissolved, with Kuwait and Saudi Arabia each absorbing half, each of the two countries still retains what amounts to half-interests in oil operations in the area.

The offshore concessions in Kuwait and elsewhere in the gulf were all developed in the post-World War II period. Prior to that time, international laws stipulated that a state could claim ownership to the continental shelf only to the extent of its territorial limits (usually three, six, or twelve miles). Since the whole gulf is a continental shelf, the question of offshore oil rights was most complicated there. In 1945 the United States extended jurisdiction over its continental shelf and soon other maritime states followed suit. The British, as the protecting power for the gulf amirates, then persuaded the rulers to claim offshore rights to a median line with Iran. The claims were never contested, but the problem of establishing a median line throughout the gulf has still not been entirely settled.

Qatar was the last gulf state to strike oil before World War II. Qatar Petroleum Company, an IPC subsidiary, obtained a concession in 1935; oil was discovered in 1939. As in Kuwait and Saudi Arabia, no oil was exported during the war. And it was not until 1949 that Qatar first began commercial production.

Subsequently, oil was discovered offshore by Shell Company (Qatar), a Royal Dutch-Shell subsidiary. In 1969, Qatar Oil Company (Japan) obtained another offshore concession, and several other companies have also been involved in Qatar. In addition, Qatar shares an oil field, Bunduq, with Abu Dhabi.

The development of oil in the UAE involved a game of musical chairs by oil company concessionaires. In 1935 Iraq Petroleum Company formed a subsidiary, Petroleum Concessions. The following year this company in turn formed Petroleum Development Trucial Coast (PDTC). By 1939 PDTC had obtained concessions from most of the Trucial States, but from then through the war, little or no exploration was undertaken. In October 1960 PDTC struck oil in commercial quantities eighty miles from Abu Dhabi town. It thereupon chose to concentrate solely on Abu Dhabi, relinquishing its concessions in the other Trucial States. The name of the company was changed to Abu Dhabi Petroleum Company (ADPC). The first exports were lifted in 1962.

Offshore rights were granted to another concessionaire, International Marine Oil Company, but it withdrew and in 1954 Abu Dhabi Marine Areas (ADMA) was granted offshore rights. Originally owned by BP (two-thirds) and CFP, Japanese interests subsequently bought a 30.83 percent equity out of BP's share. ADMA went into production in 1963.

Since then several other concessions have been granted from areas released by ADPC and ADMA. They include Abu Dhabi Oil Company (Japan), with an offshore concession that came on stream in 1973; Phillips Petroleum; Abu al-Bakush Oil Company, a French-controlled consortium with U.S. and Canadian interests; and Bunduq Oil Company. The latter, formed by BP, CFP, and Japanese interests to exploit a joint Qatar-Abu Dhabi field, is operated by ADMA.

In Dubai, Dubai Marine Areas (DUMA), a sister company to Abu Dhabi Marine Areas, obtained offshore rights in 1954. Since then, however, numerous changes have been made in ownership. DUMA came under the ownership of CFP and Hispanoil of Spain. In addition, half-interest in its concession was sold to Dubai Petroleum Company (DPC). DPC was originally owned entirely by Continental Oil Company (Conoco), but Conoco later sold 40 percent of DPC to three other firms. Conoco became the operating company. Oil was discovered in the offshore concession in 1966 and production began in 1969. DPC also had an onshore concession in 1966 and production began in 1969. DPC also had an onshore concession, but it was relinquished in 1971.

The only other oil-producing member of the UAE is Sharjah, which began production in 1974. The field, developed by a group headed by Buttes Gas and Oil Company of Oakland, California, was discovered by Occidental Petroleum Corporation, another U.S. firm with concessions in neighboring Umm al-Qaywayn and Ajman. The field was originally in Umm al-Qaywayn until Sharjah increased its territorial waters from three to twelve miles to include it. Occidental sought redress, but so far to no avail.

The other producer in the gulf is Oman. The concession for onshore oil rights was granted in 1937 to an IPC subsidiary, Petroleum Concessions, which in 1951 changed its name to Petroleum Development (Oman) (PDO). By 1960 all the IPC partners withdrew except Royal Dutch-Shell, with 85 percent, and Partex (Gulbenkian), with 15 percent. In 1967 CFP again bought in, taking 10 of Partex's 15 percent. Oil was first discovered in 1963 and commercial exports began in 1967.

OPEC

Until the 1970s, world oil prices were set by the major international oil companies. Prior to World War II, oil company efforts to regulate production and market shares in the gulf—e.g., the Red Line Agreement and the "As Is Agreement" of 1928[3] —were not designed to drive the price of oil up, as one might conclude in the post-energy crisis world. There existed a glut in the international supply of oil in the 1920s and 1930s, and the Great Depression of the 1930s compounded the oil companies' plight by drastically reducing demand. The producing countries have long charged that the oil companies conspired to keep oil prices, and hence producer-country revenues, down. But actions which have since earned the oil companies the sinister epithet of "oil cartel" were originally designed to prevent the price of oil from collapsing through cut-throat price wars. Moreover, the oil-glut mentality persisted right up to the energy crisis on 1973.[4]

The oil-producing countries chafed over what was in effect the power of the oil companies to regulate their national revenues. In 1959 a Middle East oil price cut seriously affected Venezuela, which had higher-priced crude oil. Venezuela, stung by its inability to prevent the move, consulted with Middle Eastern producer countries about the efficacy of creating a producer organization to negotiate collectively with the oil companies over price. The idea stuck a responsive chord, and in August 1960 the Organization of Petroleum Exporting Countries (OPEC) was born. Its original members were Iraq, Iran, Kuwait, Saudi Arabia, and Venezuela. In 1961, Qatar joined, and a year later, membership was extended to Indonesia and Libya. Ultimately, Algeria, Ecuador, Gabon, Nigeria, and Abu Dhabi (UAE) were also to join.[5]

At first, OPEC made little impact on oil pricing. Throughout the 1960s, a glut in supply, i.e., an excess in production capacity, maintained a buyer's market. Producing countries remembered how easy it was for the companies to increase production elsewhere in 1951 when Iran nationalized its oil. The often-heard phrase of the day in the oil-consuming countries was that the producers "cannot eat their oil."

By the late 1960s, however, increases in world demand were growing faster than increases in production capacity of both known and newly discovered oil. Another factor also became crucial. For years, the United States was the world's largest oil producer. By the 1950s, however, it was thought that U.S. production would peak by about 1970, and U.S. oil imports, mainly from the Middle East, were expected to increase rapidly. This projection proved to be correct. In other words, there were signs that the long years of a buyer's market were about to end.

Following the June 1967 war and the closing of the Suez Canal, Libya found itself in a very advantageous position because of its proximity to Europe and the low sulphur content of its oil. The Qadhafi regime, which came to power in 1969, announced production cutbacks for conservation reasons. Because Middle East oil pipelines were coincidentally closed in 1970, there was a very tight oil supply in Europe, which Libya chose to exploit. In May 1970, Occidental Petroleum Corporation, one of the smaller, independent oil companies, agreed to the Libyan government's demands for a larger government income per barrel of oil and an increase in the posted price.[6] This was the first time an oil company had given in to a producing country on price. And although Occidental was a relatively small company, its action was like a hole in the dike. By September 1970, the major oil companies operating in Libya had followed suit.[7]

The Libyan settlement sparked a succession of actions and demands by other producing countries, raising both the tax rates and posted prices, in some cases retroactively. During the OPEC conference in Caracas in December 1970, a resolution was passed specifying that, henceforth, the oil companies would negotiate oil prices with OPEC members collectively.

In the face of growing OPEC power, twenty-two oil companies, majors and independents alike, had banded together in the London Advisory Group. In January 1971, the companies, fearing that any price or other agreement not including all the producers would merely precipitate an endless spiral of increasing demands, announced that they would only negotiate with all of OPEC's members simultaneously. OPEC had come of age.

The years 1972 and 1973 witnessed OPEC's exercise of power steadily increase. Then, on October 16, 1973, OPEC unilaterally doubled the price of oil. The following December the price was doubled again. For all intents and purposes, the oil companies no longer had any role at all in establishing oil prices. In the West, OPEC was viewed as the new oil cartel, though in the classical sense of the term, neither the companies in the past nor OPEC in the present can be strictly called cartels.

OPEC is very often viewed in the West as a monolithic political-economic bloc. In fact, there are relatively few mutual political or economic interests among the members. Some are capital surplus countries and some are not; the non-Arab members do not share Arab desiderata; members are located in three continents with vastly different problems confronting them. In short, OPEC is neither a political nor an economic monolith, but a rather narrowly conceived oil-price-setting organization. The collective interest that its members have in common is to maintain the price of oil at a level well above what the oil companies had set before the 1970s. Since no member is bound by OPEC resolutions, OPEC itself does not make price decisions; the locus of power lies with the members rather than with the organization as a whole. Because nearly two-thirds of the free world's proved oil reserves are located in the gulf, the gulf members of OPEC, particularly Iran and Saudi Arabia, play a major role in OPEC decision making.

OAPEC

The Arab oil producers in the gulf also participate in another oil organization, the Organization of Arab Oil Exporting Countries (OAPEC). This organization represents a mutuality of political interests not found in OPEC. Founded in January 1968 by Saudi Arabia, Kuwait, and Libya, it was originally conceived as a conservative forum to counter more activist OPEC members, such as Algeria, Iraq, and Venezuela, as well as militant Arab states that were trying to pressure the Arab oil producers to use oil as a weapon in the cause against Israel. The Saudis in particular, while no less inimical to Israel than were other Arab states, did not want others to dictate their oil policies. Petroleum Minister Yamani, discussing the ineffective Arab oil embargo invoked as a result of the June 1967 Arab-Israeli war, said, "injudiciously used, the oil weapon loses much if not all of its importance and effectiveness."[8] Implicit in his words was the conviction that the Saudis would decide when and where it was not judicious for them to use oil as a political weapon.

Following the Libyan revolution of 1969, the conservative nature of OAPEC changed. The Libyans pressed for membership to be extended to Algeria, Iraq, Egypt, and Syria. In return, Qadhafi agreed to accept Bahrain, Qatar, Abu Dhabi, and Dubai.

OAPEC currently serves two functions. One, it is a means of distributing Arab oil money to non-Arab states, and it also attempts to coordinate economic development activity. In the latter, it is not always successful: when OAPEC decided on Bahrain instead of Dubai as the site of a regional gulf dry dock facility in 1973, Shaykh Rashid withdrew from OAPEC and went ahead with plans to build his own dry dock. In past years, OAPEC members have pledged around $80 million annually to Arab economic development, still a very small amount by Arab oil standards.

The other function of OAPEC is political. From the start it was recognized that one of OAPEC's functions was to coordinate the use of oil as a means to obtain Arab political goals. Even the Saudis accepted that premise. By 1973, King Faysal, frustrated at the lack of progress toward an Arab-Israeli settlement, was beginning to speak more emphatically of the possibility of using oil as a political tool.

The most spectacular use of oil to obtain a political objective was the Arab oil embargo of October 17, 1973, to March 18, 1974. The embargo, called in the name of OAPEC, was in fact instigated by King Faysal, who was angered at the massive $2.2 billion U.S. resupply of Israel during the October 1973 Arab-Israeli war. Faysal was able single-handedly to make the embargo effective, due to Saudi Arabia's commanding share of the world market at a time of near peak production. Iraq, on the other hand, never enforced the embargo, arguing that the embargo was only a half-way measure. Iraq nevertheless was not loath to benefit financially from not cutting its production to make the embargo work.

As it developed, therefore, OAPEC is much more politicized than OPEC, and its objectives are more broadly defined. Whereas OPEC is primarily an oil-price-setting organization, OAPEC is devoted to cooperation among Arab producers toward political as well as economic goals.

The Move Toward Nationalization

The oil-producing countries did not stop at price setting. With the exception of Iran, which technically owned its oil resources, the other producers had given up title to the oil through the concession agreements. As early as 1967, Saudi Arabia's minister of petroleum, Ahmad Zaki Yamani, had announced a scheme called "participation," whereby the producing countries would gradually buy out the producing company subsidiaries of the oil companies.

After long and difficult negotiations, the Saudis and several other producers reached an agreement with the companies for immediate purchase of 25 percent equity and ultimately full ownership of the producing companies in their respective countries. The pace of transfer of equity far exceeded the original agreement, however. By the summer of 1974, Saudi Arabia and Kuwait had increased their participation share to 60 percent, and the following year, negotiations were launched for 100 percent. As the Saudis went, so went the other gulf producers.

Production facilities were still operated by the companies, but the participating countries could dispose of their share of the oil (called "participation crude") as they saw fit. Generally they sold the oil back to the companies to market. However, the "buy-back price," as it was called, was slightly higher than the equity price—the price set on the companies' share of the oil produced. Moreover, the U.S. companies could claim no tax deductions on buy-back oil. In July 1974 the Kuwaitis further raised the price of their buy-back oil to 94.8 percent of the posted price, thus raising the actual price of oil even higher.

Iraq did not follow the participation route. In June 1972 it nationalized the Iraq Petroleum Company after years of negotiating over exploration, production rates, and other issues. The dispute with the owners of IPC over compensation was settled in January 1973, as a result of mediation efforts by the secretary-general of OPEC and an official of the Compagnie Française des Pétroles (CFP). The settlement included compensation to the owners and transfer of ownership of a sister company, the Mosul Petroleum Company, to Iraq.

Another sister company, the Basrah Petroleum Company (BPC), was not nationalized then, but as a result of the October 1973 Arab-Israeli war, the equity of the U.S. partners (Exxon and Mobil) and the Dutch partner (Royal Dutch-Shell) was nationalized as well. (The United States and the Netherlands were objects of the Arab oil embargo.) Nationalized production was transferred to the state-owned Iraq National Oil Company (NOC), which was formed in 1964. Finally, on December 8, 1975, Iraq nationalized all remaining equity in BPC.[9]

Another country to nationalize, ironically, was Dubai, which took title to all its oil operations on July 10, 1975. Dubai had spurned OPEC, dropped out of OAPEC on the dry dock issue, and had never shown any interest in participation. The nationalization of its oil, however, appears to have been a very shrewd move. Shaykh Rashid not only reaped political benefits for taking over the producing companies, but compensated the companies so well, through oil purchase credits and a management contract, that everyone appears to be happy.

When the Persian Gulf producers obtained participation agreements, the shah sought an arrangement with the consortium of oil companies in Iran to ensure that Iran would have a financial return no less advantageous than the participation countries. An agreement was signed in July 1973 whereby the consortium formed a company to produce, process, and transport Iranian oil under a five-year service contract. The Iranians will sell oil to the consortium over a twenty-year period on a cost-plus-fee basis, guaranteeing Iran the financial equivalent of participation agreements obtained on the Arab side of the gulf. Any change on the Arab side will automatically increase the "balancing margin" on the Iranian side to equalize the return.

In brief, the years 1968 through 1975 have seen the gulf producers not only gain control of their own oil resources, but also gain the power to set prices.

Future Trends and Gulf Oil Policies

Prior to the 1970s, oil supply-demand relationships were maintained in relative balance at an approximately stable price. All the parties involved were thoroughly familiar with the rules governing the producer country-oil company negotiations over production levels, taxes, and royalties. Long-run demand projections, however, nearly always erred on the conservative side. Spurred by low prices, demand for oil in the 1950s and 1960s grew at a much faster rate than expected, exhausting excess production capacity worldwide and creating the seller's market of the 1970s.

When the oil-producing countries seized the initiative in setting prices and production rates, the old stable order of supply-demand relationships was swept aside; and no new equilibrium has replaced the old. We are in effect living in an interim period between the old order and a new order yet to evolve. Much of the difficulty in the capitals of the major consuming countries in their attempts to form comprehensive energy policies arises from the uncertainty of future energy supply-demand relationships and the place in these relationships of oil.

The oil producers themselves concede that, in the long run, high oil prices will cause a decrease in demand for oil due to its costliness and, more important, due to a subsequent shift to other sources of energy. But they also point out that oil is a wasting asset, and for many of them their only major source of revenues. They argue too that they are actually doing the world a service by forcing it to develop alternative sources of energy now while oil is relatively abundant, rather than later when it is almost gone. After all, they point out, it will take years, perhaps decades to develop energy alternatives.

It is therefore the medium term, the next five to ten years, wherein lies the most uncertainty. This is reflected in the wide range of opinions among professional oil and financial men about production levels and cumulative revenues that will be accrued by the oil-producing countries by 1980. For example, the World Bank projected in 1974 that OPEC countries would accumulate $650 billion (current dollars) by 1980.[10] A year later, projections ranged considerably lower. Walter J. Levy, for example, projected $449 billion by 1980, while First National City Bank projected $189 billion and Morgan Guaranty projected $179 billion. Moreover, the gap between high and low projections was greater than the low projections.[11]

In part, the problem of projecting such figures stems from the uncertainty of future supply-demand relationships. Projections made with different price assumptions will naturally vary widely. In addition, there is little concensus on the price elasticity of the demand for oil. In other words, there is substantial disagreement on the relationship between the price of oil and the demand for oil in the medium term. Some economists are convinced that continued high oil prices are certain to lower demand, but at the cost of a world recession. The 1974-1975 recession is seen as evidence of this trend. Others, while conceding that high oil prices can be deflationary to the extent that they inhibit demand for higher-priced goods and services, do not think that high oil prices per se must necessarily bring on a depression. They point to the general expectation that the industrial economies will recover in the next few years, and project that, as a result, oil demand will rise despite high prices, The real unanswered questions in the medium term are to what degree will high oil prices affect the recovery and to what degree will the recovery affect oil demand and hence oil prices.

Another problem is estimating the supply of energy from non-OPEC sources over the medium term. Not only have high oil prices placed coal in a strong competitive position, but new supplies of oil from non-OPEC sources are expected to come into production, in the North Sea, on Alaska's North Slope, in Mexico, and elsewhere. Additionally, the higher price of oil has spurred the production of known but previously uncompetitive sources, particularly in the United States, and has stimulated oil exploration throughout the world as well.

Still another difficulty in medium-term projections lies in the overwhelming influence that policy decisions of the major producing and consuming countries will have on supply-demand relationships. Taxes, trade barriers, import and export subsidies, foreign investment policies and regulations will all bear on medium-term energy patterns. Yet, because these decisions will be made on political as well as economic grounds, there is almost no way to predict with certitude what such policies might be, much less what their effect will be.

These issues, if analyzed in depth, would take us far beyond the scope of this book. It is necessary to bear them in mind, however, as we turn now to the factors underlying oil policies in the gulf. These factors will be major determinants of oil policy making no matter what direction the actual policies may take. There are at least four such factors: 1) the desire for revenues to finance development; 2) the desire to conserve oil resources, which are a wasting asset; 3) the desire to avoid measures that would seriously undermine world economic stability; and 4) the desire to maintain control over price setting through OPEC.

Maximizing oil revenues involves a very complicated calculus. In purely theoretical terms, it entails establishing a rate of production over a given period of time that will balance the advantages and disadvantages of obtaining revenues while exhausting reserves. The calculus is different for each country, depending on capital needs and oil reserve positions. Iran, for example, has a relatively high absorptive capacity for capital expenditures, but at present production rates its reserves will be exhausted by the end of the century. It would seem to be in Iran's long- and short-term interests, therefore, to maintain high prices and limited production.

Saudi Arabia, on the other hand, has a relatively low absorptive capacity for capital expenditures and the largest proved oil reserves in the world (around 150 billion barrels). To the extent that high oil prices would encourage shifts to other forms of energy, leaving Saudi Arabia with unexploited reserves, it would seem to be in its interests to increase present production at somewhat lower prices.

In actual oil policy decision making, no country follows the dictates of such practical analysis to the degree that some professors of petroleum economics would perhaps like it to do. For one thing, a country's perception of its need for revenues and the estimation of its absorptive capacity for capital are based in large part on that country's subjective view of the urgency of the need for change in its own society. For example, in the West, building a hospital with an operating overhead of several thousand dollars per bed per day might be considered wasteful. But in a country with very few hospitals and billions of dollars of reserves, such expenditure might be considered reasonable. Most of the gulf states strongly desire rapid material and social benefits for their people, and are willing to pay double or even ten times what a similar project might cost in the West. Thus their capital "needs" tend to exceed most Western projections.

Conservation can also become a political and emotional issue as well as an economic one. Kuwait had begun conservation measures even before the energy crisis of 1973. However, the natural gas that it expects to use for its domestic industrial and private consumption is associated with its oil production. Thus, too great a cut in production, whether for conservation or to keep prices up, would also deprive Kuwait of natural gas for domestic economic development. Of the other producers, only Bahrain has a relatively high absorptive capacity for capital, at least in ministate, per capita terms. Having discovered oil early in 1932, it has a more advanced social and economic infrastructure than is the case further down the gulf. But its oil reserves are nearly exhausted. Roughly half the oil used in Bapco's refinery comes via pipelines from Saudi Arabia. Bahrain's oil policy, therefore, could not really influence international supply-demand relationships. Moreover, Bahrain is not a member of OPEC.

Of the lower gulf producers, only Abu Dhabi has significant production with projected earnings for 1976 in excess of $6 billion. Abu Dhabi's Shaykh Zayd, who is also president of the UAE, has been generous with the other UAE shaykhdoms in addition to developing his own country. Still, Abu Dhabi ranks with Saudi Arabia and Kuwait as having the lowest capacity of all the OPEC members for absorbing capital. It has a native population of less than 250,000. Most of the citizens of the UAE shaykhdoms are still at a rudimentary stage of social and economic development. Thus, development opportunities are simply too limited to absorb with even minimum efficiency, based on Western standards, the kinds of revenues Abu Dhabi is accruing. On the other hand, Abu Dhabi's generosity and largely uncoordinated foreign aid policies actually created a short-term liquidity problem in 1974-1975.

The other lower gulf producers—Dubai, Sharjah, and Oman—have smaller production levels and are quite able to absorb their revenues, even though in an economic sense they would probably be considered low-absorptive countries were their revenues as great as those of the major gulf producers.

The remaining gulf producer, Iraq, presents somewhat of an anomaly. Despite its radical regime, Iraqi oil policy has always been pragmatic and moderate. With the long and bitter dispute with IPC now finally settled, and with Iraq seeking to stabilize its political position domestically and regionally, many expect Iraq to pursue a very ambitious internal development policy and to adopt petroleum policies aimed at maximizing revenues. Some experts believe that Iraq may have revenues rivaling, if not equaling, Saudia Arabia's, and that it could develop into a major oil power, a role heretofore played within OPEC by Iran, Venezuela, and Saudi Arabia.

None of the gulf producers, nor any other OPEC member for that matter, wish to see the collapse of the free world economy. As a Kuwaiti stated the case, "We are all in the same boat. If it sinks, we go down too." This sentiment was made explicit in the Solemn Declaration made during the March 1975 OPEC Conference:

> The Kings and the Presidents. . . fully realize the close links between national development in their own respective countries and the economic prosperity of the world as a whole.[12]

There has been considerable debate about the sincerity of this producer point of view, given the deleterious state of the world economy after the four-fold price hike of 1973. It has been charged in the West that high oil prices had such an inflationary effect that they ultimately led to a recession, particularly in the United States, in 1975.

The producers, however, dispute the inflationary effect of high oil prices. According to an Iranian oil man, during the twelve-month period ending October 1973—i.e., prior to the energy crisis—consumer prices went up 6.6 percent in Germany, 8.1 percent in

France, 9.9 percent in Britain, and 11 percent in Italy. In the same period, wages rose by 12 percent, 13.8 percent, 13.9 percent, and 26 percent in the same countries. Thus, OPEC calculated that only 2 to 3 percent of the estimated 14 percent average inflation rate in 1974 could be attributable to the rise in oil prices.[13] What the producers fail to mention, however, is that while factors other than oil may contribute more to inflation, the extra margin of inflation created by higher oil prices may turn out to be, if the reader will excuse the metaphor, the straw that breaks the camel's back.

It is evident that, although the producers tend to absolve themselves of the major responsibility for the state of the world economy, they do not wish to see it weakened. It was due to concern over the destabilizing effect of the sudden price rises on the world economy that caused Saudi Arabia to express the desire in the summer of 1974 for lower oil prices. That in the end the Saudis did not lower prices unilaterally, despite their ability to do so, was more the result of not wishing to disrupt OPEC and Arab solidarity than of a lack of concern over the effect of the high prices.

The gulf producers, as indeed all OPEC members, are absolutely insistent that they retain the power to set prices and production levels through OPEC solidarity. Some experts believe that, with new, non-OPEC oil coming on stream, that solidarity cannot survive. During the softening of demand in 1974-1975, they point out, Saudi Arabia almost unilaterally had to cut production to keep prices up, since countries like Iran had to maintain both high production and high prices to fund their ambitious development plans. At the point where the Saudis balk at bearing the burden for cutting production to maintain prices and call on the others to cut back on a prorated basis, these experts feel that OPEC solidarity will end. In the words of one State Department official, it will "bust up the OPEC cartel."

These predictions appeared to some to be borne out in December 1976 when Saudi Arabia and the UAE refused to go along with an OPEC 15 percent price rise, 10 percent immediately and 5 percent in July 1977. The Saudis and the UAE contended that the rise was too high and raised the price only 5 percent. By July 1977, however, a compromise had been worked out to restore a single price whereby the Saudis and the UAE raised their prices 5 percent and the other OPEC members cancelled the additional 5 percent raise. Thus, the "two-tier" price system, as it was called, turned out to be a temporary situation which, while certainly straining OPEC relations, proved that OPEC was capable of withstanding such strains. Predictions of OPEC's demise, at least for the present, appear to be wishful thinking.

In addition to the obvious economic incentive to work together through OPEC, there is an added psychological dimension. It is difficult to measure the psychological impact of the events of 1973 and 1974 on the OPEC members, but it does appear to be great.

After years of feeling impotent in oil dealings not only with the major oil companies but the major consuming countries as well, some of whom had been their colonial masters, the oil producers could not help but reap a great sense of satisfaction if not downright glee at being able to turn the tables and make the consuming countries squirm. Political solidarity cannot be based on such emotion, but it does appear to have strengthened the oil producers' determination to maintain a common front no matter what market forces portend.[14]

In addition, it costs only thirty cents a barrel to produce oil in the gulf, whereas much of the new oil, in Alaska and the North Sea, will cost many times that to produce. The OPEC-gulf countries will therefore still have a strong competitive advantage.

Thus, if market conditions do force a moderation of oil prices in the middle term, and there is considerable uncertainty that they will, OPEC can probably sustain a considerable diminution of its current economic power before it ceases to function as a collective force in price setting. Moreover, in order to maintain solidarity OPEC members would probably agree to moderate prices before they ever reached the point where Saudi Arabia would demand prorating production cutbacks. Algeria's President Boumedienne reflected OPEC's determination to control prices when he said, "If prices have to be frozen, we will freeze them. If they must be decreased, we will decrease them."[15]

Whatever OPEC's future, the gulf producers will play a leading role in international oil relations for the forseeable future. Having two-thirds of the free world's proved reserves, it cannot be otherwise.

NOTES

[1]The text of the concession appears as an appendix to Annex 1419c. in the League of Nations *Official Journal* 13 (1932): 2305-2307. The D'Arcy concession was actually preceded by a broader concession including rights of exploration for all minerals except gold and silver, awarded to a naturalized British citizen, Baron Julius de Reuter, in 1872. Its provisions were restricted in 1889, and the entire concession was declared void by the Persian government in 1901. See George Stocking, *Middle East Oil: A Study in Political and Economic Controversy* (Nashville, Tenn.: Vanderbilt University Press, 1970), pp. 3-8.

[2]He is often referred to as "Mr. Five Percent." See Ralph Hewins, *Mr. Five Percent: The Story of Calouste Gulbenkian* (New York: Rinehart and Company, 1958).

[3]This so-called agreement was made by representatives of Jersey Standard (Exxon), Royal Dutch-Shell, and Anglo-Persian (BP) during a weekend grouse hunt at Achnacarry Castle, England. It was intended to fix market shares among the companies just as the Red Line Agreement attempted to regulate supply. See the Federal Trade Commission, *The International Oil Cartel*, published by the Select Committee on Small Business, U.S. Senate, 82nd Congress, 2nd Session (Washington, D.C.: Government Printing Office, 1952). Also mentioned in Stocking, *Middle East Oil*, pp. 84-85.

[4]For example, see M.A. Adelman, "Is the Oil Shortage Real? Oil Companies as OPEC Tax Collectors," *Foreign Policy* 9 (Winter 1972-1973): 69-107. Professor Adelman took a conspiratorial view that the oil companies sought in league with the producers to create a shortage in order to raise prices, despite abundant proved reserves.

[5]Although the UAE membership technically includes all three oil-producing shaykhdoms, only Abu Dhabi is an active participant. Dubai and Sharjah have never shown any interest in OPEC.

[6]The "posted price" was an artificial accounting price per barrel for computing taxes on the producer companies and royalties on the oil they produced. It was generally higher than the actual price the companies paid. Moreover, since the U.S. companies were allowed to deduct the foreign taxes from their U.S. tax liabilities, the cost of the oil to the companies was in effect even less, by the amount of their U.S. tax write-offs, than the price they paid.

[7]The so-called major oil companies, or Seven Sisters, are Exxon, Mobil, Socal, Texaco, Gulf, Royal Dutch-Shell, and BP. In addition, CFP of France is sometimes considered a major. The other companies are called "independents."

[8]*Middle East Economic Survey*, July 21, 1967.

[9]*New York Times*, December 8, 1975.

10See Robert McNamara's Annual Address to the World Bank reprinted in the *Summary Proceedings of the 1974 Annual Meeting of the Board of Governors,* p. 31.

11See Richard D. Erb, "The Financial Management Problem From the Perspective of OPEC Members," unpublished paper delivered to the Council on Foreign Relations, July 11, 1975.

12The text of the Solemn Declaration was published by OPEC in the *Washington Post,* March 18, 1975, p. B-16.

13See D. Reza Fallah, "The Energy Crisis: Its Origins and Suggested Remedies," address delivered before the Centre International d'Etudes Monetaires et Bancaires, Geneva, Switzerland, Nov. 28-30, 1974.

14This theme was developed from my paper, "The Politics of OPEC," presented to the Council on Foreign Relations in New York on April 24, 1975.

15*Washington Post,* March 3, 1975.

6
Economic Prospects
in the Gulf

The economic structure of the gulf is the result of the impact of oil revenues upon the widely diverse traditional economies of the gulf countries. Preoil economic activity centered around five principal activities: agriculture, animal husbandry, commerce and trade, fishing, and pearling.

Agriculture was limited largely to well-watered areas such as the Caspian Sea coast in Iran, to irrigable river valleys such as the Tigris and Euphrates, to those mountainous areas that had both sufficient rainfall and soil for terrace farming, and to scattered oases. Animal husbandry was the principal occupation of nomadic tribes inhabiting the mountains of Iran and Iraq and the great deserts of Arabia. In the field of commerce, the gulf area lay astride the major trade routes from Europe to the Orient. One branch extended overland through Iran to India. The other moved by sea from the Persian Gulf to India and Africa. The gulf also provided a livelihood for fishermen and pearl divers. Pearling was a major industry in many of the gulf shaykhdoms before the cultured pearls from Japan captured most of the trade.

Another important economic activity was religious tourism. Before the discovery of oil, the cash economies of Saudia Arabia, and its predecessor the Kingdom of Hijaz, consisted almost entirely of receipts from the annual *hajj* to Mecca and al-Medinah.

Pilgrimages to Shi'a Muslim shrines such as the tombs of Hassan and Husayn in Karbalah, Iraq, were also important economically, albeit in lesser scale than the *hajj*.

All of these pursuits are still present to a lesser or greater degree throughout the gulf area. The coming of oil, revolutionary as it has been to the local economies, did not initiate a totally new way of life. Rather, it began the transformation of the old, a process for which there is still no end in sight.

The economic prospects of the gulf states depend on their own individual sets of circumstances, and no two states are exactly the same. But for all states, the primary determinant of economic growth potential is oil. Because there is so much uncertainty over projected oil revenues in the middle term, however, there is an equal amount of uncertainty in trying to project growth potential.

The Structure of the National Economies

As we have noted in the previous chapter, there are great differences in both the reserve positions of the various gulf states and in their absorptive capacities for development capital expenditure. To analyze fully the economies of any single gulf state would be a major undertaking all its own. The following are but brief descriptions of these economies.

Iran

With a large population and land mass, Iran has the base to develop a modern, productive economy. Its population, projected to be 36 million by 1978, is growing at roughly 3 percent a year. Although a large part of its 636,000 square miles (1,648,000 square kilometers) is arid, there is still much potential for increasing the productivity of arable land.

Iran has a free market economy dominated by the public sector. The oil industry, of course, provides the major source of revenue to promote economic growth. Beginning in 1948, the government initiated a number of development plans aimed at modernizing the economy. The first two (1948-1955 and 1955-1962) experienced difficulties, due first to the period of instability and loss of oil revenues during the Mussadiq period, and also to the lack of managerial expertise within the public sector. Nevertheless, agricultural productivity was increased, the social and economic infrastructure was greatly upgraded, and the stage was set for the impressive growth rate begun in the 1960s and sustained to the present.

The Third Development Plan (1962-1968) became the cornerstone for the rapid economic development of the 1960s and 1970s. Moreover, the impetus created by government investment spurred private investment so that it actually exceeded investment in the public sector throughout the period of the plan.[1] In agriculture, extension of irrigated lands, construction of wells and dams, and improvement of farming techniques were instituted, but the main accomplishment was in land reform.

The Fourth Development Plan (1968-1973) was designed to concentrate on the industrial sector, but continued to give attention to balanced growth in all sectors. The current Fifth Development Plan was inaugurated in March 1973 and is expected to continue to 1978. Originally, it was to involve a total expenditure of $35.5 billion, greater than that of all the previous years combined. But with the oil price rises of 1973-1974 vastly increasing revenues, the plan was revised to produce an expenditure of $68.6 billion.[2] This should greatly increase the expected growth rate under the plan beyond the originally projected 14 percent; but because of fluctuations in the world economy since the 1973-74 energy crisis, it is difficult to project what the real growth figure will be.

The political expression of economic development is the White Revolution, which the shah evolved during the 1960s.[3] In late 1961 he declared by royal decree a program which became the first six of Twelve Points for Progress of the Revolution of the Shah and the People. The heart of the program was land reform. In January 1962, after the shah himself had ceded all personal property and business interests to the nation through the Pahlevi Foundation, he instituted the Land Reform Act which was to give land tenure to the largely landless Iranian peasants. By 1967 nearly 1 million farmers held title to their lands.[4]

On January 26, 1963, the six points—land reform, nationalizing forest lands, sale of equity of state-owned factories to the private sector to raise revenues for land reform, a provision for sharing with the workers 20 percent of the net profits of industrial establishments, creation of a Literary Corps, and universal suffrage— were passed by public referendum. Between 1963 and 1977, 13 more points were added. These included creation of a Health Corps, a Development and Agricultural Extension Corps, and a Legal Aid Equity Corps. Other points called for nationalization and development of water resources, urban and rural reconstruction, and reform of the civil service.

Agriculture still dominates the Iranian economy in terms of the labor force. In 1971 some 3.4 million out of a total labor force of 8 million were engaged in farming, forestry, hunting, or fishing.[5] Some 60 percent of the population still live in rural areas.

Despite the great strides in modernization and land reform, the agricultural sector is still largely underdeveloped. Nearly 90 percent of all Iranian farmers are estimated to live at a subsistence level.[6] While crop levels have steadily increased over the past years, much of the increase can be attributed to increases in the land under cultivation, particularly irrigated land.

The Fifth Development Plan places particular emphasis on agriculture, partly because a rapidly increasing population has made shortages in domestically produced foodstuffs a growing problem. The first stages of land reform (1962-1967) concentrated on redistribution of land tenure. Since then, concentration has been on increasing farm mechanization and on consolidating fragmented holdings. In the Fifth Plan, farmers are being induced to join cooperatives for better efficiency, and agricultural credit is being extended. In addition, public sector agro-industrial projects are being planned, including joint ventures with foreign partners.

Forestry in Iran had not been economically productive before nationalization in 1963, and many former forests were denuded and prevented from growing back by overgrazing livestock. The Forestry Commission now supervises conservation and reforestation efforts that should make wood products a more important resource. Some 11.5 percent of Iran is currently classified as woodlands.[7]

With the exception of the caviar industry in the Caspian Sea, fishing is also very underdeveloped in terms of its potential. However, Iran is now focusing more attention on building up its fishing fleet. One survey estimated that a potential income of $200 million annually could be earned from a more developed fishing industry.[8]

It is through industrialization that the shah hopes to build Iran into an economic (and political) power. Assuming that oil resources will be available only for domestic use by the turn of the century, Iran is undertaking a major industrialization program which it hopes will match West Germany's productive capacity by that time. Special emphasis is being placed on the petrochemical industry as a means of maximizing revenues from oil and gas resources. This industry began with the opening of a fertilizer plant in Shiraz in 1961. The Fifth Plan projects a growth rate of 22 percent per year in the petrochemical industry. By 1983 Iran hopes to meet 5 to 10 percent of world demand for petrochemicals, including fertilizers, plastics, and other products.[9]

To insure markets and gain technology, the government is encouraging joint ventures with such U.S. firms as DuPont, Allied Chemical, and Dow Chemical as well as with European and Japanese firms. Iran's National Petroleum Company (NPC), a subsidiary of NIOC, is the principal public sector investor in petrochemicals. NPC hopes to concentrate on basic production, leaving intermediate and final processing to the private sector.

Iran is also expanding its iron and steel industry. The first steel mill, Arya Mahr, was established at Isfahan with Soviet credits first extended in 1965. The plant began production in 1973. Operated by the National Iranian Steel Corporation (NISCO), it is Iran's second-largest employer, following the oil industry.

Iran hopes to expand its steel-producing capacity from 2 million tons in 1972 to 15 million tons by 1982. NISCO plans to invest about $6 billion in expansion and hopes to generate another $2 billion from the private sector and foreign sources. One scheme is to set up a 3-million-ton per year plant at Bandar Abbas in an Iranian-financed venture with Italy's Finsider Corporation. Unlike the Isfahan mill, this would obtain iron ore from abroad, possibly from India. This mill would turn Iran into a net exporter of iron and steel.

Symptomatic of Iran's foreign investment policy was the announcement on July 17, 1974, of its acquisition of 25 percent interest in the steel works of Germany's Krupp.[10] Krupp needed Iranian capital, and Iran in turn hopes to utilize not only Krupp's markets but, perhaps more important, its technical expertise for Iran's own steel industry.

There is also a growing automotive industry in Iran. The first assembly plant was established in 1957 and by 1973 production reached 51,000 cars, 6,300 trucks, 5,000 busses and minibusses, and 14,300 delivery vans. This accounted for all but 8 percent of Iran's internal demand.[11] With the rising standard of living and protective import restrictions, demand is expected to grow even greater. It has already outstripped supply and is creating horrendous traffic problems, as any pedestrian in the auto-clogged streets of Tehran can verify.

The largest of twelve auto producers is Iranian National, which produces a domestic version of a Hillman, called the Peykan, under license from Chrysler (U.K.). To date, most of the components of the Iranian auto industry must be imported, but Iran National has launched a $100-million project to build its own engines and ultimately hopes to produce an all-Iranian car.

In addition to these enterprises, Iran is pushing ahead with development of a social and economic infrastructure on a broad front. Rail, all-weather road, and air links are being expanded. New hydroelectric projects are being planned and constructed, and in February 1974 Iran ordered five nuclear power stations from France at a cost of around $1.2 billion.

Iraq

Despite the radical socialist coloration of the Ba'thist regime, Iraq still has a mixed economy with an active private sector. Because of political-economic constraints on the private sector and the fact that oil revenues and economic planning are in the hands of the government, however, the public sector should continue to dominate the Iraqi economy.

Like Iran, Iraq has an oil-based economy and a largely agricultural society. In ancient times, a highly sophisticated system of irrigated farming existed in Mesopotamia ("the land between the rivers"), but the Mongol invasions of the thirteenth through sixteenth centuries virtually destroyed it, and it has never fully recovered. Nevertheless, over half the labor force is engaged in farming.

Economic-development planning began with the creation of a Development Board in 1950, and the first Five Year Plan was adopted in the following year. When the monarchy was overthrown in 1958, the Development Board was abolished and planning was undertaken first by the Ministry of Development and later by a newly created Ministry of Planning.

Between 1951 and 1970, numerous "five year plans" were adopted, but their average life span was only two years.[12] This rather spotty performance was attributable to a combination of technical and political factors. Initially lacking in technical expertise, early projects were often ill devised and poorly administered.

In the monarchical period, an attempt was made to develop the economy while leaving the traditional land-owning aristocracy largely intact. While many real gains were made, particularly in controlling the flood-prone Tigris and Euphrates rivers, the planners did not sufficiently take into consideration the social revolution of rising expectations going on in Iraq. The monarchy was overthrown in a bloody revolution in 1958.

Succeeding regimes in Iraq have continued the planning efforts begun earlier. Their plans, however, reflecting their socialist political orientation, have followed Soviet designs; and, indeed, Soviet technicians have helped prepare them. During the 1960s, development was greatly inhibited by political instability, exacerbated by periodic Kurdish insurgencies. It was also impeded by stagnation of oil revenues due to disputes with the oil companies and later with Syria over the IPC pipeline from Iraq to the Syrian port of Banias on the Mediterranean.

By the 1970s, the Ba'thist regime that had gained power in 1968 had achieved a measure of internal stability. This was enhanced by the rapprochement between Iraq and Iran in early 1975, causing the latest Kurdish insurgency to collapse. Moreover, Iraq resolved its dispute with the oil companies in February 1973, and later in the year its oil revenues increased dramatically as a result of the four-fold price increase. Thus, by mid-1975 Iraq possessed the political stability and financial resources necessary to embark on a major program of development.

Prior to 1970, economic planning had concentrated primarily on the agricultural sector. The 1970-1974 plan and the current 1975-1979 plan, however, place an equal focus on industry as well. Moreover, both reflect the quantum jump in revenues. The 1975-1979 plan calls for an investment in agriculture and industry of around $5 billion.

The agricultural sector is inhibited by land tenure practices, lack of education among the farmers, and undercapitalization. Post-1958 regimes have attempted to deal with the land tenure problem through land reform, and the original land reform measures virtually stripped the landed aristocracy of their large holdings. However, being more politically inspired than based on economic feasibility, these measures actually decreased productivity.[13]

Land tenure is still complicated in Iraq, with free holds, religious-endowment (*waqf*) land, public land, and three kinds of government tenure. Gradually, however, reform is taking hold. Over 400,000 farmers have received land, and agricultural cooperatives have been established. Increasingly, the government is turning to collective farms both for political and pragmatic reasons, but collectivization is being done mainly in newly reclaimed areas rather than areas already under cultivation.

Of Iraq's 172,000 square miles (443,000 square kilometers), roughly half is arable. Of this, only about one-fourth is under cultivation. Thus, with intensive capital investment, Iraq can increase its agricultural production manyfold and probably support a population of over twice the present 11 million. The main problems are to increase the educational level of the farmers, introduce better methods and mechanization, and expand capital infrastructure such as dams, canals, and adequate drainage to prevent salination. And ultimately, an Euphrates waters agreement must be worked out with Syria and Turkey. In the spring and summer of 1975, Iraq charged that Syria had cut the flow behind its new Euphrates dam and caused severe hardship to Iraqi farmers.[14] Though it is doubtful that the issue will lead to an open confrontation between Iraq and Syria, it looms as a potential problem which could seriously affect Iraq's agricultural development.

Industry, with the exception of oil, has never been a key factor in the Iraqi economy. Nevertheless, with vastly increased revenues, the Iraqis now wish to balance their agricultural sector with a strong industrial sector. Although industrial growth has increased by 7.5 percent a year for the past twenty years, it still represents only 10 percent of the gross domestic product and employs only 8 percent of the labor force.[15] Larger enterprises were nationalized in 1964, and future large-scale investment will be made by the government.

Iraq hopes to base its industrialization around its own natural resources, moving from production of raw materials to intermediate processing, and ultimately to final processing. Thus, agro-industry and petrochemicals will receive primary attention. Economic infrastructure, such as power and communications, and import-reduction projects will also be developed.

During the lean years of the 1960s, much Iraqi development was financed by the Soviets. Now that it has sufficient oil revenues, Iraq is turning more to the free world market place to obtain high-quality goods and services. While not allowing foreign investment in Iraq, the regime is anxious to contract for completed "turnkey" projects and service contracts with a training component for Iraqis.

Saudi Arabia

The Saudi economy is one of the most laissez faire in the entire gulf. The strict and conservative Hanbali school of Islamic law followed by the Saudis is surprisingly liberal on most business practices. As an example of the strength of free market philosophy, Saudi merchants regularly do business with all the major communist states, while politically the government refuses to establish any diplomatic relations with these states and one cannot even place a telephone call from Saudi Arabia to the communist world. Despite its strident capitalism, the Saudi economy is totally dominated by the public sector, by virtue of the commanding position of the oil industry.

The development philosophy of Saudi Arabia was first enunciated by the late King Faysal. Basically, it was his intention to provide for his people a twentieth century material way of life while preserving an Islamic social order developed a milennium ago. Education, social welfare, and economic development were all stressed, but strictly within the context of Islamic social values. The evolution of Saudi society can thus be seen as a head-on collision of modern technocratic ideas and ancient socio-religious beliefs.

Development projects are carried out by the various ministries and other agencies. Because each is jealous of its prerogatives, cooperation among them is sometimes hard to attain. For example, at a time when no communications network existed in Saudi Arabia, no less than four independent systems were being designed—by the Communications, Defense, and Interior ministries and the National Guard.

Comprehensive government planning first began to gain acceptance in 1968. In February of that year, Shaykh Hisham Nazir was appointed to the previously moribund Central Planning Organization (CPO). With the technical assistance of U.S. and other consultants, the CPO produced Saudi Arabia's first development plan, for 1970-1975. Although it had been estimated that the plan would provide for an annual GDP growth rate of 9.8 percent, this ultimately proved too high. Originally, some 41.3 billion in Saudi riyals (SR) in expenditures was allocated to the plan, but after the 1973-1974 price rises, it was expanded by 35 percent. The main aim of the plan was to diversify Saudi Arabia's single-commodity economy. Agricultural development and industrialization, particularly in petrochemicals, was stressed, along with infrastructure projects.

In mid-1975, the Second Five Year Plan was announced. With a massive $149 billion allocated for expenditure, it continued along the same lines as the first plan. The magnitude of the plan reflects the vast increase in Saudi revenues, but given the growing economic bottlenecks in the region generally, many observers doubt that the plan can be fully implemented in five years.

Before the discovery of oil, Saudi Arabia was primarily an agricultural country, but its agricultural development potential is relatively restricted. Farming is limited to scattered oases, the largest of which is the great al-Hasa (al-Ahsa) Oasis; to a narrow strip along the Hijaz Mountains; and to (usually dry) stream beds flowing from those mountains. Out of some 830,000 square miles (2.15 million square kilometers), only some 1 million acres, or 0.2 percent, are under cultivation.[16] Most of this is date palm orchards. Nearly all of the livestock consists of subsistence nomadic herding.

Despite limited agricultural potential, some expansion is possible. In the 1960s a major study was made of water resources, leading to a program for digging wells and mining archeologically stored water in the deserts. Four major agricultural projects were also begun: a land irrigation and drainage scheme at al-Hasa; construction of a dam at Wadi Jizan on the Red Sea; another dam near Abha, the capital of Asir; and a Bedouin settlement and land reclamation project at Haradh.

The al-Hasa irrigation and drainage scheme was completed in 1971, after five years of work. Costing some SR260 million

($57.7 million according to the exchange rate at the time), it reclaimed 12,000 hectares of land that had grown saline through years of irrigation without proper drainage. The project is estimated to provide a livelihood for some 50,000 persons.

The King Faysal Model Settlement scheme was completed in 1972 at a cost of SR100 million. The project area has a capacity to re-settle 10,000, but the government has experienced difficulty in persuading proud and independent Bedouin to locate there. The nomadic tribesmen much prefer the freedom of wandering through the desert as whim and weather lead them.

The Wadi Jizan Dam was completed in 1971 as a first step in a larger project to develop irrigation throughout the entire valley. Costing SR42 million ($9.3 million), it has the capacity for 71 million cubic meters of water storage. The Abha Dam, completed in 1974 at a cost of SR29 million, has a capacity for 2.4 million cubic meters of water. In addition to these projects, an agricultural school has been opened at Buraydah, and a nationwide well-drilling project is being conducted.

A major boon to agricultural expansion is the growing demand for foodstuffs as Saudi Arabia's standard of living grows. Over 60 per-cent of the country's needs must be imported. Continued capital-ization of the agricultural sector and opening up the relatively fertile Asir to domestic markets through the construction of all-weather roads will greatly enhance domestic production. However, the gap between local supply and demand will probably continue to grow.[17]

Although Saudi Arabia was basically an agricultural country prior to the exploitation of its oil resources, the main foreign exchange earner was the *hajj*, the annual Muslim pilgrimage to Mecca and al-Medinah. Compared to oil income in 1974 of nearly $27 billion, the economic importance of the *hajj* is now negligible. Neverthe-less, the *hajj* still comprises the most important commercial season in Saudi Arabia, and the *hajj* service industry, both public and private, employs a large proportion of the labor force, if on no more than a part-time basis.[18] It has been estimated that over a third of all consumer-related transactions are made within the six- to eight-week *hajj* season. Thus, for Saudi Arabia the *hajj* has roughly the same commercial impact as the Christmas season in the United States. Wholesale and retail inventories are stocked in anticipation of this key selling season.

Most goods sold to *hajjis* are imported, thus reducing the economic impact of sales. Nevertheless, when considering the income-generating effect of *hajj* commercial activity, coupled with that of the annual *hajj* infrastructure and administrative expenditures made by the Saudi government, one can begin to realize its economic importance.[19] Gross *hajj* receipts probably exceed $100 million per annum, an amount equalled by government spending. Thus, the total income generated each year by the *hajj* is in the neighborhood of a quarter-billion dollars. If the number of pilgrims continues to rise, as it has in recent years, the economic and commercial impact of the *hajj* will become even greater.

The Hijaz, with its long history of *hajj* commerce, has traditionally supplied Saudi Arabia with its merchant class. There was, nevertheless, a commercial center in the Najd also. The area of Qasim had long been a key stop on the trans-Arabian caravan route, and an extensive market grew up there including one of the country's largest camel markets. Some of Saudi Arabia's leading merchant families trace their ancestry back to Buraydah and 'Anayzah, the two leading (and rival) towns of Qasim. Today the larger merchant families have branches in all the major towns, so that it is becoming increasingly difficult to talk about a single region like the Hijaz as the Saudi commercial center. For example, the capital, Riyadh, is becoming equally important, particularly for international transactions.

Aside from the oil sector and the *hajj* service industry, Saudi Arabia's industrial sector is comparatively small. The country simply lacks the natural resources and manpower to develop a large-scale industrial base. Most non-oil-related industrial enterprises are small and keyed to local consumer demand. The largest is the construction industry, which is transforming the skylines of the country's major cities seemingly before one's eyes.

The chief instrument for industrial development in the public sector is Petromin, a public corporation established under the Ministry of Petroleum and Minerals in 1962. Petromin has invested in a steel-rolling mill in Jidda; established an oil refinery, also in Jidda; and, together with the Occidental Petroleum Company, established the Saudi Arabian Fertilizer Company (SAFCO) in the Eastern Province. The latter began operating in 1969, the first two in 1968.

The primary focus of Petromin, particularly since the oil price rises of 1973, is petrochemicals. In 1974 it initiated studies for a $3 billion gas-gathering and liquefaction complex. Most of the expected 5.2 billion cubic feet per day of gas that it hopes to utilize is currently being flared in the desert. In addition, Petromin, in partnership with U.S., European, and Japanese interests, is planning a multi-billion-dollar gas-based steel plant and petrochemical installation. Oil refinery capacity is also to be expanded, with new installations planned possibly in Riyadh and Jubayl. Unlike Iraq, which prefers outside interests merely to provide technology for wholly Iraqi-owned enterprises, Petromin wishes to interest foreign partners in an equity share. In that way, it hopes to maintain higher performance levels and utilize its partners' market potential.

Industrial expansion by the private sector, which up until now has invested less development capital than the public sector, is being encouraged with favorable financing and guaranteed markets. General Motors is currently constructing an assembly plant in partnership with Saudi private interests, and expects to market its production of autos and trucks in large part to the government. Saudi private capital is also moving into fishing, shipping, and other opportunities.

One other enterprise is worthy of mention. Saudi Arabian Airlines not only provides transportation within the kingdom but is a major international carrier as well. Started in 1945, it was guided by Trans World Airlines, which still has a management contract. Saudia, as it is now called, was originally founded to provide air service for pilgrims journeying to Mecca, and, as the national Saudi carrier, it has a favorable position in chartering *hajj* flights. In recent years it has built up the largest fleet in the Middle East.

Kuwait

Kuwait looked to the sea for its livelihood prior to the discovery of oil. Before the Japanese developed cultured pearls, pearling was a major Kuwaiti industry. In 1912, Kuwait had a fleet of 812 pearl boats manned by 30,000 divers.[20] Kuwaiti shipwrights gained a reputation for making some of the best dhows in the gulf, and Kuwaiti mariners aboard those dhows developed commercial ties throughout the Indian Ocean. At home, the great Kuwaiti families developed into a mercantile class. But the coming of oil has changed all that. Even Kuwaiti fishing boats are now manned mostly by foreigners.

Because of the scarcity of fresh water, there is practically no agriculture in Kuwait. The government has an experimental farm and hopes to develop hydroponic techniques. Animal husbandry is encouraged, and there are dairy and poultry farms in the private sector. There is also a plan to use treated sewage to create a greenbelt of trees around Kuwait City. By and large, however, Kuwait will always be dependent on imports to feed its people.

Fishing is more promising, being the second-largest foreign exchange earner after oil. There is a good market for gulf shrimp and prawns in the United States, Europe, and Japan. In 1972, four fishing companies merged to form Kuwait United Fisheries, thus increasing their efficiency. The government, to encourage fishing, plans to construct a new fishing port.

The government also encourages industrial diversification, and a new industrial area has been developed at Shuaiba, south of Kuwait City. The Kuwaitis are concerned that the country be adequately prepared economically when the oil, its only major resource, runs out. In 1972, conservation measures were adopted restricting maximum production to 3 million barrels per day (bpd). Current reserve estimates (70 billion barrels) would permit production for another seventy years or so at the 1974 rate of 2.6 million bpd.

A major constraint on Kuwait's limiting production too greatly, even if it does not need the revenues, is that most of the natural gas with which it hopes to develop domestic industry and serve local energy needs is associated with oil production. As a result, the Kuwaitis have had to do some rethinking on priorities for oil and gas production.

An Industrial Development Committee aids in the expansion of local industry. The private sector is chiefly involved in consumer production and construction, which, as elsewhere in the gulf, is booming in Kuwait. The public sector is focusing, not suprisingly, on petrochemicals. As early as 1963, the Petrochemical Industries Company was formed to produce fertilizers. In 1964 it created a subsidiary, the Kuwait Chemical Fertilizer Company. With a new fertilizer plant at Shuaiba, owned by Kuwait National Petroleum Company (KNPC), the national oil company, Kuwait has become the Middle East's largest producer.

More recently, a government holding company, Kuwait Oil, Gas and Energy Company, was created to oversee the development of

Kuwait's petrochemical industry. A huge new liquid propane gas plant is in the planning stage, and there are studies for constructing an aluminum smelting plant using natural gas. In these ventures Kuwait welcomes foreign investment, particularly where contributions in technology are involved. Majority control, however, must remain in Kuwaiti hands.

In addition to diversification in petrochemicals, Kuwait also seeks to increase sales of refined petroleum products relative to crude oil exports. There are currently three refineries on stream, and KNPC, which owns one of then, is considering construction of a fourth.

One other industry, which has drawn Kuwait full circle to its seafaring days, is its modern merchant marine, one of the largest in the Middle East. The privately owned Kuwait Oil Tanker Company has been in operation since 1958 and has orders to expand its fleet. Kuwait is developing a substantial dry cargo fleet as well.

As of old, Kuwait continues to be a commercial center, and many of its imports are reexported. In addition, the Kuwaitis have developed an expertise in banking second to none in the gulf. Kuwait could be a major regional banking center were it not for its prohibition of foreign banking operations located in the country; even with this restriction, it is an important banking and capital center.

The Kuwaitis foresee returns from capital investments, handled through their own banks and investment firms, as a major source of national income when the oil runs out. Already, it is estimated that Kuwait earns over $1 billion a year from its investments and reserve holdings. The desire for a return on investments as a means of preserving the national wealth sometimes cuts across Kuwait's well-organized foreign aid program, since aid programs are not generally very profitable. While sincerely desirous of aiding other countries, questions of equity and profitability can sometimes become factors in its aid policies.

Bahrain

Among the oil-producing countries of the gulf, Bahrain is something of an anomaly. It has a balanced and diversified economy and the most advanced economic and social infrastructure found among the gulf shaykhdoms. Bahrain's educational system, first developed in the 1920s, is today one of the best in the gulf. Bahraini men of letters are known throughout the Arab world. Despite these advantages, Bahrain faces a somewhat uncertain future because of the rapid depletion of its oil reserves.

A thirty-three-island archipelago, Bahrain is small in area—130 square miles (370 square kilometers)—and only 9 percent of the land is arable.[21] Because of relatively plentiful water resources, however, Bahrain has a highly developed agricultural sector. Vegetables, fodder, and dates are grown, and cattle breeding is widely practiced. The government maintains an experimental farm. Bahrain's agricultural sector faces a long-term problem, however, for if industrial water use in Bahrain and adjacent Saudi Arabia continues to expand, the water table may drop too low in the next decade to support agriculture.

Commercial fishing is also a major industry in Bahrain. Operations range from individual fishermen to the Bahrain Fishing Company. The latter, established in 1966 by British and Bahraini interests with a capitalization of $840,000,[22] exports shrimp and prawns to the United States, Europe, and Japan.

Industry naturally centers around oil. Although the wholly owned Awali field is almost exhausted, Bahrain shares ownership with Saudi Arabia of the Abu Safa field, with over 6 billion barrels in reserves. Moreover, Bahrain has a large new field of non-oil-associated natural gas, which can be exploited industrially as well as exported. Thus, while Bahrain will never be a major oil producer, it is relatively assured of a moderate income to sustain its economic development.

The large Bapco oil refinery and the Aluminum Bahrain (Alba) aluminum-smelting plant comprise the two major Bahraini industries other than crude oil production. The Bapco refinery uses Bahraini oil and also Saudi crude which is brought in by pipeline. In addition, a new desulfurization unit with a capacity for 50,000 bpd was inaugurated in 1973. Most of its production is shipped to Japan.

The aluminum plant, which is 27.5 percent owned by the Bahraini government, went into production in 1970. It was the first gas-fired aluminum-smelting plant in the gulf, and now several other countries are considering similar projects.

Another major industrial project is the OAPEC-financed dry dock, now under construction. When completed, the Arabian Gulf Repair Yards will be able to repair tankers up to 375,000 tons.

Bahrain also has some potential as a regional commercial and communications center. It has an earth satellite station. Its new airport, opened in 1971, is capable of handling jumbo jets, and Bahrain has become a major stopover point between Europe and the Orient. Gulf Aviation, now the collective national carrier of the lower gulf shaykhdoms and Oman, was originally established with participation by BOAC, the Bahraini government, and Bahraini private interests; its corporate headquarters in the gulf are still in Bahrain. The Bahraini merchants have long-established connections throughout the region, enabling them to carry on an extensive reexport trade. The principal deterrent to Bahrain's becoming a regional commercial center is its relatively limited financial resources when compared to the major gulf oil producers.

Qatar

Located on a barren peninsula, before the discovery of oil Qatar had little or no agriculture. And unlike the other gulf shaykhdoms, it had never developed an *entrepôt* trade. Pearling, nomadic herding, and subsistence fishing were its principal economic activities.

Oil revenues, which reached $1 billion in 1975, are drastically changing the way of life in Qatar. The government, particularly since Shaykh Khalifa came to the throne in 1972, has endeavored to diversify the economy to the greatest extent possible. From practically no agricultural production in 1960, Qatar now grows enough vegetables to feed its population of 115,000, and actually exports some to neighboring countries.

Industrial development and diversification are also being planned. A number of key expatriates, such as the U.S.-educated Egyptian economist Mustafa Hassan, play key roles in development planning and investment policy formation.

Qatar has a fertilizer plant, in production since 1973, and a shrimping industry, the Qatar National Fishing Company. There is also the Qatar National Cement Manufacturing Company, and the privately owned but government-protected Qatar Flour

Mills Company. In early 1975, plans were announced that a steel mill, to be fired by natural gas, would be constructed by Japanese interests. In addition, Qatar is investing in infrastructure projects such as roads, electric power, desalination, and harbor expansion to enable it to catch up with the rest of the gulf.

The United Arab Emirates (UAE)

The economy of the UAE is the least integrated among all the gulf states. On the one hand, there is the dichotomy between the traditional, largely subsistence economy and the modern, oil-based cash economy. On the other, there is the lack of integration among the economies of the seven federation members.

Abu Dhabi is by far the wealthiest, earning more than $7 billion in 1974. Dubai has a lucrative *entrepôt* trade which had brought prosperity even before oil was discovered. Sharjah, the former commercial center of the lower gulf before it was eclipsed by Dubai, is the third UAE member to find oil, going into production in 1974. The other four shaykhdoms are practically devoid of natural resources and can only break out of their subsistence economies through the generous assistance of their wealthier neighbors, particularly through the efforts of the UAE president, Shaykh Zayd.

Most of the social and economic infrastructure projects in the UAE are carried out by the federation government. Owing to Dubai's lack of financial support for the union budget, these projects are funded almost entirely by Abu Dhabi. Roads and schools in particular are being built at a rapid pace. Dubai and Sharjah, having the resources, are also undertaking extensive development projects within their own borders.

Economic planning is still at a rudimentary stage both at the federal and amirate levels. Abu Dhabi launched a five-year National Plan in 1968 with estimated expenditures of $662 million. But due to a lack of administrative expertise, inflation, and other factors, expenditures were outrunning revenues and the 1969-1970 budget was reduced by 35 percent. More recently, problems in planning and coordination of its generous foreign aid program caused Abu Dhabi to experience a short-run cash liquidity problem in early 1975, despite huge revenues in that period. Presently, with the aid of foreign consultants and advisors, a start is being made to plan and coordinate government expenditures.

The agricultural sector in the UAE can be expanded to some degree, but because of a general lack of water, its potential is limited. Abu Dhabi is attempting to increase productivity in the Buraymi (al-Ayn) Oasis, where an experimental farm was established in 1968, and in the Liwa Oasis. It has also established an Arid Lands Research Center on Sidayat Island, staffed by the University of Arizona. The greatest potential for agricultural development, however, lies in Ras al-Khaymah and along the Batinah Coast on the Gulf of Oman. Ras al-Khaymah has an experimental farm at Diqdaqqa, established by a dedicated Briton, Robin Huntington, in 1955. It is now a federation school offering a three-year course for anyone from the UAE with at least six years education.[23] There is also a more recent experimental farm at Dhayd, in Sharjah. The Batinah Coast, on which are located Fujayrah and enclaves of Sharjah, has a narrow but relatively fertile strip of land which can be exploited to a much greater extent when the new paved road now under construction connects this region with the rest of the country.

Animal husbandry is primarily limited to the nomadic Bedouin. Dairy farming has been introduced in Ras al-Khaymah with a new breed of cattle, but it is only a start. In irrigated farming areas, tick-borne diseases are especially dangerous to livestock.

The fishing industry has somewhat more potential. Natives of the UAE, as of Kuwait and Bahrain, were traditional seafarers, fishermen, and pearlers. Although pearling has all but disappeared, and gulf shrimp and prawns cannot be found as far south as the UAE, fishing is still an important occupation. In Ajman, 27 percent of the working population are fishermen, and in Umm al-Qaywayn, 460 fishermen represent 30 percent of the work force.[24]

However, fishing in the UAE is still relatively primitive. Fishermen use many types of craft, from small *shashar* made of palm trees to diesel-powered fishing dhows holding up to forty men. Traditionally, most of the catch not sold locally was dried and sold in East Africa and South Asia, but these are no longer lucrative markets. Still, the fishing industry could be vastly expanded with the purchase of a modern fleet, and with canning and freezing facilities ashore. A fishmeal industry might also be feasible. A study by the Food and Agriculture Organization (FAO) showed abundant fish resources in the lower gulf and even more so in the Gulf of Oman. The FAO recommended a high priority be placed on developing a commercial fishing industry for export.

The industrial sector dates almost entirely from the discovery of oil in the early 1960s. The rate of development since then has been impressive. Abu Dhabi, which had no paved roads in 1962, is a modern city with dual highways, a waterside drive, and modern sewage, electricity, and other facilities. The modern airport and port facilities are again being expanded.

Abu Dhabi will undoubtedly follow the example of other major oil producers with heavy public sector investment in capital-intensive export industries utilizing its oil and gas. A $3 million liquid natural gas (LNG) plant is being constructed at Das Island, and plans call for a $2 billion LNG processing complex at Riways by 1980. Abu Dhabi is also considering a steel-rolling mill and an aluminum smelting plant.

Attention is also given to consumer and construction industries. Abu Dhabi already has a flour mill and is constructing a cement plant at Abu Dhabi town and at al-Anin. In the private sector, a number of small consumer-oriented industries have grown up in Abu Dhabi. A major factor inhibiting their growth, however, is the small market in the UAE. Abu Dhabi has a population not greater than 100,000, and the UAE as a whole about 350,000.

Dubai, the commercial center of the lower gulf, concentrates its development on expanding its commercial interests and service industries. Several modern luxury hotels have just opened or are planned, and Dubai has an ultramodern airport which is being expanded. Port Rashid, a modern facility with sixteen berths, was completed in 1972 for about $70 million. Shaykh Rashid now wishes to expand the facility into a huge free port. Not satisfied with OAPEC's choice of Bahrain for a dry dock facility, he is building his own, which will be capable of handling a million-ton (deadweight) supertanker and a ship half that size at the same time. Dubai's infrastructure projects include two new bridges over and a tunnel under its "creek" (the estuary which forms the heart of its traditional port), an international communications system including an earth satellite station and an automated telex exchange, and a color television system.

It is difficult to distinguish between the public and private sectors in Dubai, so intertwined are family business interests with local government interests. As a result, Dubai's free market economy is one of the least restricted in the world. "Free trading," including smuggling of gold and luxury items to Iran and South Asia, still remains an important element in the economy. During a recent visit, I was told of private merchants interested in purchasing a launch capable of exceeding sixty knots per hour, presumably for free trading activities.

Neighboring Sharjah, now receiving oil revenues, is also attempting to diversify and expand its industrial sector. One of its first projects is to construct a deep-water port, although Sharjah town is only about ten miles from Dubai. Sharjah has a cement factory, as does Ras al-Khaymah, and is also constructing modern hotels.

Were it not for the UAE's location at the farthest end of the gulf, it could have some potential as a banking center. Its currency was unified in 1973 with the creation of a UAE dinar; a central bank was created; and thirty-nine banks are licensed, including major U.S., British, and Middle Eastern firms. The banks have been authorized to construct 250 branches throughout the country, and had opened about 150 by mid-1975. According to an official of the UAE Currency Board, there is now a moratorium on foreign banks, although it is still possible to establish a joint venture with 80 percent local equity.

Oman

Prior to the discovery of oil, fishing and agriculture were the principal forms of economic activity in Oman, and they still employ over 80 percent of the labor force. Although the first oil shipments were made in 1967, almost no efforts at economic development were undertaken until 1970, when Sultan Qabus replaced his father in a bloodless coup. Since then, development has almost become a matter of trying to do everything at once. By early 1975 government expenditures had so exceeded revenues that Oman experienced a severe short-run cash liquidity problem, which was eased by a timely loan of several million dollars from Saudi Arabia. Since then, the government has had to slow the pace of development expenditures and consolidate the gains already made.

Oman has had a very large defense burden owing to the insurgency in Dhufar. The government, however, seems to have gained the upper hand. Moreover, with the oil price increases of 1973, its economic picture is a bit brighter. Nevertheless, Oman probably never will be a major oil producer.

The agricultural sector still operates largely at a subsistence level. About 36,000 hectares are under cultivation. Since rain is sparse and unpredictable, there is very little dry farming except in Dhufar. In the interior, there are terrace farms on the mountain slopes. In the oases at the foot of the mountains, water is tapped and transported to the fields by means of underground canals known as *aflaj* (singular: *falaj*). On the Batinah Coast the fields are irrigated by deep wells. Most of the crops are planted beneath date palm groves. In Dhufar, on the other hand, there is too much rainfall for dates, and coconut groves are plentiful instead.

The government has concentrated a considerable investment in upgrading the agricultural sector. In November 1970 it created a Department of Agriculture under the Ministry of Development to coordinate its efforts in northern Oman. Two experimental farms established by the British, one at Nizwa in 1959 and one at Sohar on the Batinah Coast in 1962, have been augmented by two more farms. By the end of 1972, sixteen agricultural extension centers were established in the north. Five water resource surveys are also being conducted in northern Oman by international consultants as a basis for future planning.[25]

In Dhufar, agricultural development is conducted through the Department of Agriculture of the Dhufar Development Department, established in 1971. It maintains an experimental farm at Salalah for growing cattle fodder, and a U.S. firm, Farm Machinery Corporation (FMC), which has a $6 million contract to establish experimental and demonstration farms, has another fodder-growing farm near Salalah.

FMC is also working on animal husbandry projects both in northern Oman and Dhufar. There are an estimated 190,000 head of livestock in northern Oman, but due to diseases and poor blood lines, the quality is poor. At Sohar, a small beef and poultry project is under way. In Dhufar, the government hopes to upgrade the livestock of the cattle herders who live in the insurgency-ridden mountains. Part of the problem is to induce the herders to sell male calves for beef rather than butchering them as is the usual practice.

The fishing industry currently engages about 10 percent of the work force. Omani fishermen traditionally dried and salted the fish they could not sell locally and sold them in East Africa and South Asia. Currency restrictions have cut into those markets; and due to the rise in the standard of living, many Omanis no longer care for dried fish.

The Omani government, therefore, has set about to increase the market potential for small fishermen through creation of refrigeration and processing facilities and also hopes to develop a large-scale modern commercial fishing industry.

In 1972 a Fisheries Department was established under the Directorate-General of Industries of the Ministry of Development. Two firms, Mardela and Del Monte, were granted contracts to develop the fishing industry. Recognizing the need to develop managerial skills, two Omanis were sent to Britain to study fisheries management.[26]

In Dhufar, fisheries are being developed by the Ministry of Development in cooperation with the Dhufar Development Department. Storage and marketing facilities are being built and local fishermen are being provided with small boats and outboard motors. By all reports, both the Batinah Coast and Dhufar have a great potential for a lucrative commercial fishing industry.

Traditional handicrafts comprised the only industries in Oman prior to 1970. In September 1972 a Department of Industries was created under the Ministry of Development. The department has requested technical assistance from the United Nations Industrial Development Organization (UNIDO) in industrial planning, encouragement of small businesses, and preservation of the handicrafts industries.[27]

Oman has centered its efforts for large industry on three areas: cement, oil refining, and petrochemicals. A cement plant with a capacity for 600,000 tons a year is scheduled for completion in 1976. The Department of Petroleum and Minerals is considering the feasibility of a refinery. And a gas pipeline to the capital is being planned as a first step toward the development of a petrochemical industry.

Problems and Prospects

There can be no doubt that oil revenues are rapidly changing the economies of the gulf states. The rate of change will be conditioned by future oil revenues and by the other resources each country can exploit for development. In assessing future economic prospects in the gulf, there are five potential problem areas with which all the states must cope: manpower resources; administrative and physical infrastructure including communications and transportation; market forces as they affect imports and exports other than oil; non-economically productive expenditures such as military purchases and foreign aid; and investment of petrodollar reserves.

The *shortage of manpower* is potentially the most critical bottle-neck to development throughout the gulf. The problem has two dimensions. The first relates to a single country's manpower resources as compared to the financial resources it can devote to development. While able to finance large programs, most gulf states except Iran have a very small population base. The problem is doubled since, as a result of Islamic social mores, only about 2 percent of the female population is employed.

Not only is the availability of manpower limited, but educational levels are low and traditional attitudes antithetical to the develop-ment of a modern technological society are prevalent. Bedouin, for instance, generally refuse to do menial tasks. Illiterates are unable to perform the highly sophisticated tasks required in many development schemes. Moreover, many of what are considered menial tasks in the West require a degree of literacy difficult if not impossible to obtain among blue-collar workers in the gulf. Even Iran, with a population of 33 million, expects to create several thousand jobs in present development plans for which there will be no qualified Iranian workers. Great emphasis is being placed on education, but raising the general level of education re-quires decades, and few gulf states are willing to wait that long.

Yet another aspect of the domestic manpower problem is the paucity of qualified leadership. In most gulf countries, major decisions are made by only a handful of persons. Because of the ambitious nature of the development policies, the demands on their time are staggering. Often progress on a project is halted be-cause a key official has not had the time to make the necessary decisions.

The second dimension of the manpower problem is related to foreign labor. Thus far, the gulf states have been able to overcome manpower shortages by hiring expatriates. Kuwait and the UAE both have more resident aliens than natives, and one out of every five inhabitants of Saudi Arabia is a foreigner.

Present figures for foreign labor, however, do not reflect the quantum jump in development goals since 1973. It is estimated that by 1980 there may be over a quarter-million U.S. citizens in the gulf. As the number of foreign laborers grows, many states will have to consider the political and security impact of so many alien residents, many of whom are placed in key jobs.

In addition, many surrounding states with no oil income, which have traditionally exported skilled and semiskilled labor to the gulf, will find shortages themselves. These shortages could be further exacerbated if foreign aid from the oil producers creates jobs at home for the same skilled workers whom the oil producers are trying to hire.

Despite language and cultural problems, the gulf states will have to seek further afield for manpower if they are to maintain projected rates of economic growth. Indians and Pakistanis of all classes are flocking to the lower gulf. Pakistani doctors and veterinarians have been working for a number of years in Saudi Arabia. If economic conditions deteriorate in Europe, it is possible that expatriate European workers might enter the gulf labor market.

Inadequate administrative and physical infrastructure has long been a major bottleneck in the gulf. Port congestion, primitive internal transportation and communications, and time-consuming administrative procedures have plagued nearly every project attempted in the area. Of all the problem areas, however, the most progress has been made in this one. New or expanded ports, airports, and roads are completed or under construction everywhere. Communications systems, including telex and earth satellite stations, are making the gulf accessible from anywhere in the world. There has also been a degree of administrative reform. Clearing customs, obtaining work permits, and other procedures are becoming far more efficient, largely due to the pressure of large-scale business operations involved in development projects.

At the same time, it is doubtful whether the improved administrative procedures and new facilities can cope entirely with the vastly expanded development projects now being planned. One measure of the boom atmosphere is the availability of hotel space. Despite hotel construction throughout the gulf, rooms are fully booked months in advance and many distinguished but shortsighted visitors end the day sleeping on a sofa in a hotel lobby.

Market forces are the great unknown of gulf economic development. World inflation, not unrelated to high energy costs, is driving up the price of goods and services that the gulf states must import in order to implement their development plans. Inflation is also carrying over into the domestic economies, a growing cause for concern among the gulf states. The cost of development must constantly be revised upward.

Another key issue is future world demand for nonoil production. None of the gulf states except Iran has a sufficiently large population base to create a significant domestic market, and even Iran is concentrating on export industries. The problem is that all of the gulf states have roughly the same resources—oil and gas, but few others. Each state plans to develop its own petrochemical industry, and several are planning steel and aluminum plants. There has been little regional economic coordination, and if all these plans are implemented, there could develop a huge glut in supply. Fertilizer demand is notoriously fickle, for example, and as new plants come on stream, the price is almost certain to be undermined. For those states with such industries already in operation, however, it would be very difficult, for political reasons, to halt production and lay off workers. In anticipation of such a possibility, Kuwait has quietly abandoned the idea of a steel industry. Without more regional planning or research into entirely new products for petrochemicals, industrialization in the gulf could turn out to be a burden rather than a boon to the local economies.

Non-economically productive expenditures are hard to assess in an economic context since their justification is based primarily on noneconomic considerations. Moreover, most such expenditures have some economic value. For example, upgrading military capability entails training programs and acquisition of skills, much of which eventually carries over into the private sector.

Military transfers to the gulf have received much attention in the last few years as purchases began to escalate sharply. Although most of the debate over what is a reasonable level of arms purchases has centered on strategic and political considerations, the argument is also made frequently that defense expenditures deny funds for economic development.

With the exception of Oman, which has been fighting a major insurgency, there seems to be little convincing evidence to support this contention, at least since the increase in oil prices in 1973.

Most gulf states can buy both guns and butter. Moreover, even if states with large military budgets, such as Iran and Saudi Arabia, were to divert defense funds to economic development projects, the resulting increase in the rate of economic growth would not be greatly accelerated, due to the slow pace at which these funds could be productively absorbed.

Military programs do, however, retard economic growth to the extent that they compete with the civilian sector for trained manpower. And in the case of Iran, should oil revenues begin to decline, some hard decisions would have to be made on priorities. Iran is stretching its resources to the limit in order to maintain its ambitious military and economic development programs at the same time. Since 1972, Iran has ordered over $8 billion in arms from the United States alone.

Another possible non-economically productive expenditure is foreign aid. Abu Dhabi's recent liquidity problem is an example of how insufficiently coordinated aid programs can adversely affect domestic economic development. Other gulf states have generally extended foreign aid in the form of low-interest loans. And some development loans actually involve equity holdings by the lender. At any rate, were oil revenues to contract markedly in the gulf states, foreign aid would undoubtedly be the first to suffer.

There is one other major area of nonproductive expenditure in the gulf, the extra "fees" extracted by agents and even government officials in return for services in obtaining a contract. In the eyes of the West, these practices are considered unethical and a drain on the local economies. From an ethical standpoint, they may indeed be deplorable. However, as with military expenditures, they harm the economy only when the government cannot afford the loss of such resources and still sustain economic growth. In countries with large surpluses, such practices actually aid in distributing the national income by means of a "trickle down" system. Tolerance of graft in high places is easier when it can be accomplished in low places as well.

The *accumulation of petrodollar reserves* also has two dimensions. First is the impact of large reserve holdings in the gulf on the world economy. Early in the energy crisis, fears were raised that by the 1980s the OPEC producers would hold hundreds of billions of dollars of reserves, creating a world capital shortage and forcing the industrialized countries to go hopelessly in debt. Thus, the concept of "recycling" these reserves back into the world economy was born.

The initial fears have proved to be greatly exaggerated. Reserve holdings have not increased as fast as earlier projections, and some gulf producers actually expect to be net borrowers by 1980. Also, the international banking system has been able to manage the huge transfers of capital resulting from the oil price rises.

Investment of petrodollars is still a problem area, however. Economic dislocations resulting from the 1973 oil price rises have had a deleterious effect. For example, many countries have run up large balance of payments deficits as a result of higher oil bills. As a rule, the gulf producers have avoided becoming directly involved in these kinds of problems. Proposals for lower oil prices for net debtor countries, or for low-interest, long-term loans to ease payments problems, have not met with enthusiasm from the producers. Instead, they have let the international banking system and world market mechanisms make the adjustments. Several have made loans to the International Monetary Fund as an indirect means of easing payments problems.

In terms of their own investment policies, the producers, particularly the Arabs, have been very loath to make long-term investments and in some cases have actually paid negative rates of interest on short-term deposits. The banking system is not able to absorb such large amounts on a sixty- or ninety-day basis. In addition, since large-scale movements of short-term monetary assets could be very disruptive both politically and economically, there has been a general suspicion in the West of gulf investment intentions. This suspicion in itself has had a negative economic impact.

The other dimension is the impact of capital investment on the states themselves. To a great degree, the monetary assets now being accumulated will have to substitute for oil resources as the latter become depleted. Iran and Iraq hope to utilize most of their oil incomes in developing their domestic economies. Others, while also stressing economic development, have less domestic economic potential and will be required to make more foreign investments. The best investment opportunities are in the industrial world. Kuwait and Saudi Arabia have also explored a triangular arrangement that would utilize their money and Western technology for development projects in the nonoil Arab states such as Egypt, Sudan, and Yemen. Here again, trade-offs must be made in the returns on investment, since development projects do not generally bring a high return.

Each gulf state will approach these problem areas in different ways. The political and economic variables affecting their success are so numerous that it is essentially impossible to predict the outcome. To a great extent, however, their futures depend on investment choices made today.

NOTES

[1]American University, *Area Handbook for Iran* (Washington, D.C.: U.S. Government Printing Office, 1971), p. 372.

[2]*The Middle East and North Africa 1974-1975: A Survey and Reference,* 21st ed. (London: Europa Publications, 1975), p. 333.

[3]See Pahlevi, H.I.M. Mohammad Reza Shah, *Mission for My Country* (New York: McGraw-Hill, 1961), and Pahlevi, *The White Revolution* (Tehran, 1967).

[4]Charles Issawi, in Ehsan Yar-Shater, ed., *Iran Faces the Seventies,* Praeger Special Studies In International Economics and Development (New York: Praeger, 1971), p. 55.

[5]*Middle East and North Africa,* p. 334.

[6]*Ibid.,* p. 327.

[7]*Ibid.,* p. 328.

[8]*Ibid.,* p. 329.

[9]*Ibid.*

[10]*New York Times,* July 18, 1974, p. 1.

[11]*Middle East and North Africa,* p. 332.

[12]Albert Y. Badre, "Economic Development in Iraq," in Charles A. Cooper and Sydney S. Alexander, eds., *Economic Development and Population Growth in the Middle East* (New York: American Elsevier Publishing Company, 1972), p. 288.

[13]See Rasool M.H. Hashimi and Alfred L. Edwards, "Land Reform in Iraq: Economic and Social Implications," *Land Economics* 37 (Feb. 1961): 75, quoted in Badre, "Economic Development in Iraq," p. 296.

[14]*Washington Star,* May 22, 1975, p. A-20.

[15] Badre, "Economic Development in Iraq," p. 223.

[16] Since not all the borders are delimited, an exact figure for land area cannot be given. For figures on arable land, see *Middle East and North Africa*, p. 593.

[17] Edmund Y. Asfour, "Saudi Arabia, Kuwait and the Gulf Principalities," in Cooper and Alexander, *Economic Development and Population Growth*, p. 381.

[18] For a discussion of the administrative and economic aspects of the *hajj*, see David E. Long, *The Hajj Today: A Survey of the Contemporary Pilgrimage to Makkah* (doctoral dissertation, George Washington University, Washington, D.C., Feb. 1973).

[19] The Saudi Budget figure for *hajj* expenditures in 1974-1975 was only SR243.8 million ($70 million); but this does not include *hajj*-related expenses accruing to nearly every other ministry. For example, the Foreign Ministry must handle a huge volume of visas and also care for VIP pilgrims; the police must provide security and traffic control; the Health Ministry must provide sanitary measures; and so on.

[20] American University, *Area Handbook for the Peripheral States of the Arabian Peninsula* (Washington, D.C.: U.S. Government Printing Office, 1971), p. 116.

[21] Muhammad T. Sadiq and William P. Snavely, *Bahrain, Qatar, and the United Arab Emirates: Colonial Past, Present Problems and Future Prospects. Studies in International Development and Economics* (Lexington, Mass., Toronto, and London: Lexington Books, D.C. Heath Company, 1972), p. 46.

[22] *Ibid.*, p. 58.

[23] K.G. Fenelon, *The United Arab Emirates: An Economic and Social Survey* (London: Longman, 1973), pp. 49-50.

[24] *Ibid.*, p. 58.

[25] Sultanate of Oman, Ministry of Development, National Statistical Department, *Development in Oman, 1970-1974* (Muscat, Oman, 1975) p. 17.

[26] *Ibid.*, p. 29.

[27] *Ibid.*, p. 35.

7
The United States and the Gulf

Direct U.S. interests in the gulf originated in Oman in the 1820s. At that time, the sultanate was a leading maritime power in the Indian Ocean. Muscat, the capital, was one of the great ports of the Indian Ocean; and Zanzibar, a dependency of the sultan, was the center of the slave trade, both East and West.

In the winter of 1827-1828, a New Hampshire merchant, Edmund Roberts, seeking to recoup losses in South America, arrived at Zanzibar. Incensed at discriminatory import and export taxes levied on U.S. vessels, he sought an audience with the sultan. The latter asked him why the United States did not conclude a commercial treaty with him, a suggestion Roberts took back to the United States.

In 1832 Roberts was empowered by the State Department to negotiate commercial treaties with Cochin China, Siam, and Muscat. In order not to arouse the suspicions of the British over the nature of his mission, he sailed on the U.S.S. *Peacock* as the captain's clerk.[1]

Roberts was an able negotiator. On one occasion, when he discovered the esteem in which titles were held, he reeled off after his own name the names of the counties of New Hampshire.[2] Arriving in Muscat in 1833, he negotiated a Treaty of Amity and

Friendship that remained in force until it was replaced in 1958 by a new Treaty of Amity, Economic Relations and Consular Rights. The treaty was ratified by the U.S. Senate on June 30, 1834, and Roberts returned to Muscat the following year to exchange ratifications. As it turned out, Roberts the merchant was never to reap the benefits of Roberts the negotiator. Contracting dysentery in Siam, where he had also exchanged ratifications, he died in Macao in 1836 en route to Japan.

The treaty with Muscat provided for the appointment of a U. S. consul. Richard Waters, a Salem merchant, became consul in Zanzibar in 1837. The following year a New York merchant arrived at Muscat, but left soon after, and a British subject was appointed consul. In 1843 the position went to Said bin Khalfan, the translator of the 1833 treaty.

By the mid-nineteenth century, Oman's commercial importance had waned drastically. Slavery had been a major economic activity, but in 1822 the sultan concluded with Britain the Moresby Treaty enjoining him from further trade. In 1861, Zanzibar, the major slaving port of East Africa, was lost altogether.

In 1909 the United States decided to assign a full-time consul to Muscat. Two events had intervened. First, trade had increased measurably between Muscat and the United States as the latter became one of the chief importers of Omani dates. By 1907-1908, the value of U.S. imports from Muscat, £43,000, was second only to that of India.[3] Within a few years, however, the date trade began to decline considerably due to competition from California dates and to changing American tastes. And after 1914, World War I generally disrupted communications and trade in the area. With the death of the consul in 1915, the consulate at Muscat was closed. Not until World War II would there be a full-time official U.S. representative in the gulf.

The second event that encouraged the appointment of a full-time consul was the establishment some years before of an American Protestant Mission in Muscat. The missionaries had appealed to the U.S. government to intercede with Muscat over impediments being placed in their way by the local authorities.[4]

Though small in number and outside the mainstream of politics and commerce, the American missionaries in the gulf have contributed as much as any other group to the creation of cordial relations with the United States. To many residents of the gulf, the missionaries were the first and in some cases the only regular contact with Americans. Unlike traders and the imperial representatives of the European powers, the missionaries came to give, not to take from the gulf. Their generosity and love have created an image of Americans in the gulf that even the vicissitudes of politics and the Arab-Israeli conflict have not destroyed. Their sons, as those of other missionaries in the Middle East, became the first generation of post-World War II American "Arabists," in government, business, and academia.

The Arabian Mission of the Reformed Church in America was founded in 1889 by the Reverend Samuel M. Zwemer and the Reverend James Cantine. Zwemer, who was later known as the "Apostle to Islam," became a noted scholar of Islam and Arabic. A small mission station was established in Basrah in 1892 and another in Bahrain in 1895. The mission in Muscat was opened in 1893, and in 1910, arrangements were made to open a mission in Kuwait. A mission station was also opened at Amarah, Iraq.[5]

Within a short time, the missionaries realized the great need for medical services and incorporated medical work as one of three focuses: medicine, education, and evangelism. The modern schools and hospitals established by the missionaries were the first such facilities in the gulf.

The early years of the Arabian Mission were a less sensitive age than the present. The missionaries established close relationships with the gulf leaders of the time and often performed services far beyond their normal responsibilities. The Reverend Dr. John Van Ess, for example, contributed to the World War I effort by producing the first modern text of Iraqi colloquial Arabic at the request of the British Military Government in Basrah. The book subsequently became a classic of its kind.

Dr. Van Ess was also named acting U.S. consular agent in Basrah in 1914 when the war created a need for an official U.S. representative there. Both during and after the war, his efforts and informal advice were invaluable and helped pave the way for U.S. recognition of Iraq in 1931.

During his tenure as consular agent, Dr. Van Ess even got involved in a "spy incident," which his wife relates in an amusing reminiscence.[6] When the consulate at Muscat was closed in 1915, its effects, including a small box labeled "Consular Jewels," were shipped to Basrah. Subsequently, a lady traveler bound for

Baghdad stopped at Basrah, being unable to continue due to the fighting. "Mrs. Johnson," as she called herself, was taken in by a missionary family, but soon the British became suspicious of her. A Major Gregson had her searched and questioned, but, other than secret pockets in her corsets and sun helmet and a hollow heel in a shoe, could find nothing incriminating. She was a thoroughly hardened individual of indeterminate age and origin who teased him for not himself searching her person. "I wouldn't have minded, I am not deformed!" she said, much to the Victorian gentleman's embarrassment.

It was later deduced that she was a German spy sent to obtain the Muscat "Consular Jewels," for they had turned out to be the State Department code book. Not only had Van Ess already burned the book by then, but "Mrs. Johnson" further made the mistake of staying with the wrong missionary family. For her efforts, she spent the rest of the war as an internee in India.

Through the years, the educational and medical needs of the gulf states changed. State educational and medical facilities obviated the need for the missionary facilities. In some cases, the missionaries decided to close hospitals and schools. In others, they were asked to do so by the host governments. The hospital at Amarah, Iraq, was forced to close by the government after the 1958 revolution. On the other hand, the Shaykh of Bahrain has expressed his desire for the missionary presence to stay on.

The palace coup which brought Sultan Qabus to the throne in Oman in 1970 presented a new challenge to the American missionaries. Previously, theirs were the only hospitals available to Omanis in the country. (The oil company and British Consulate had private medical facilities.) Shortly after coming to power, Qabus wrote to the American mission:

> In recognition of the humane and invaluable assistance, which by the selfless endeavor of your Mission has been available to our people in such generous measure over the years, we wish to inform you of our gratitude in the past, and open support in the future.[7]

Despite such warm support, however, the missionaries had to decide whether to continue until the newly organized Health Ministry could supply adequate medical services, at which time the mission hospitals no longer would be needed. This had been the pattern elsewhere in the gulf. The other alternative was to offer the mission hospitals to the Health Ministry as a base on which to develop, for in fact the ministry had no existing facilities at all.

There was a division of opinion among the missionaries about whether working for the government would help or hinder their primary mission of Christian evangelism. In the opinion of the writer, it is a mark of farsightedness on the part of the Reformed Church that they elected to donate their facilities and services to the government. In that way, the government obtained an instant program and utilized the missionaries' long experience, and the missionaries participated in the ground-floor discussions and planning in the Ministry of Health.[8]

Beginning on January 1, 1971, the property of the Arabian Mission hospitals was leased to the Ministry of Health for one Omani riyal a year (then about $2.50). The missionary staff of the hospitals donated their services to the ministry and remained in charge of the administration of the hospitals. The ministry, for its part, financed all medical services provided at the hospitals.[9] Three years later, the properties were donated outright to the ministry, excepting a house and a small chapel. Members of the mission's medical staff, including members of the Danish Missionary Society who had joined in the medical work in 1965, were all seconded to the Ministry of Health without pay. They are still there serving their God and the people of Oman. In recognition of their labors, Dr. Donald Bosch, who became the administrator of the new government hospital at al-Khuli, was awarded the "Order of Oman" in 1972.

The other long-term influential American presence in the gulf has been the oil companies. Chapter 5 has outlined briefly how and when they came. The economic and technological impact of the oil companies should be obvious. Until local government services were developed, the oil companies, like the missionaries, had to create their own. Aramco, for example, built its own schools, hospitals, roads, and other facilities. Creation of these facilities in many cases laid the original groundwork for services which the government has since been able to provide its people.

There is also a human dimension. Oil company personnel provided the first, daily contact of many gulf citizens with products of a Western, secular society. Many deep and lasting personal relationships were developed which transcended oil company business. It was common, for example, for gulf leaders to seek the advice of oil company officials on a wide range of issues, on a purely personal basis. Perhaps the conviction of many in the gulf that U.S. technology and methods are the best in the world stems from long experience with U.S. oil companies and their American personnel.

The Evolution of U.S. Policy in the Gulf

In the present day, the paramount U.S. interest in the gulf is oil. Interest in oil entails concern for its price and availability. It also entails concern for regional political stability and security in order that oil price and availability not be changed precipitously for political or military reasons. A derivative economic interest is in the investment policies of gulf states with large petrodollar reserve holdings. The accumulation of large reserves constitutes a major redistribution of world economic wealth; and without careful thought to investment policies, severe economic dislocations in the world economy could result. Commercial interests in the gulf, therefore, can be seen not only as opportunities to increase sales, but also in terms of the beneficial effect that the sale of U.S. goods and services to the gulf states has on the U.S. balance of payments.

Despite these obvious economic, political, and strategic concerns, the gulf did not become a specific area of policy interest until 1968, when the British announced their intentions to disengage. Prior to that time, the United States had developed close bilateral relations with a number of gulf states, notably Iran and Saudi Arabia. Sizable arms sales and military training programs had been developed with both countries. The United States has also maintained a small naval facility in the gulf since 1949, the Middle East Force (MIDEASTFOR), which consists of a flagship and two destroyers assigned on a rotational basis. Nevertheless, oil policy was left largely to the British, who maintained an army base at Sharjah and a navy base at Bahrain.

The initial U.S. reaction to the British decision to disengage was one of dismay. It was perceived by many that the British withdrawal would threaten the security and stability of the region by creating a "power vacuum." Unless this so-called vacuum were filled by the West, there was considerable concern that the Soviet Union would attempt to fill it, either directly or through support of Iraq, seen as a Soviet client state. The dilemma, as it was perceived, was that the U.S. public, sharply divided over U.S. involvement in Vietnam, would not support any U.S. efforts to undertake the British security role in the gulf. This sentiment was reflected in a statement by Senate Majority Leader Mike Mansfield the day after the British announcement:

> I am sorry the British felt they were forced to take this step because I am certain we will be asked to fill the vacuum east of Suez. I don't know how we are going to do it because I don't think we have the men or resources for it.[10]

U.S. policy in the gulf as it developed after 1968 attempted to reconcile U.S. concern for the security of the area with the judgment that the U.S. public would not support a direct security role there. The emphasis on security in overall U.S. gulf policy was reflected in a statement of "five principles" by the then assistant secretary of state for Near Eastern and South Asian affairs, Joseph Sisco, in September 1972:

1. Non-interference in the internal affairs of other nations.
2. Encouragement of regional cooperation for peace and progress.
3. Support for friendly countries in their efforts to provide for their own security and development.
4. Encouragement for the principles enunciated in the Moscow Summit of avoiding confrontations.
5. Encouragement for international exchange of goods, services and technology.[11]

The first three principles provided the conceptual framework for a policy of political support and indirect security assistance with a minimum U.S. presence beyond the military training missions already in place in Iran and Saudi Arabia. The policy relied heavily on cooperation between Iran and Saudi Arabia and became known informally as the "two pillar policy," or in a broader context, "regional cooperation." It also relied on close cooperation with the British, who were expected to continue to play a major, though in time diminishing, internal security role in Oman and the gulf shaykhdoms.

The October 1973 Arab-Israeli war had a profound effect on the gulf. The shaykhdoms, long isolated from the rest of the Arab world during the years of British protection, found themselves drawn inescapably into Arab world politics and the Arab-Israeli conflict. When King Faysal announced the Arab oil embargo in reaction to the $2.2 billion U.S. military resupply to Israel, all the gulf producers except Iraq supported it.

Bahrain, moreover, terminated the agreement providing homeport facilities for MIDEASTFOR which it had enjoyed since 1949. The Bahrainis had always been ambivalent in their attitude toward MIDEASTFOR. On the one hand, they welcomed the U.S. military presence as a form of visible U.S. support for the regime. On the other, they felt vulnerable to political attack for allowing a foreign military presence on Bahraini soil. Upon attaining independence in 1971, the government agreed to MIDEASTFOR's staying on; but in the wake of the October 1973 Arab-Israeli war, the one-year termination clause was invoked.

This decision was later reversed, and a new agreement was signed in July 1975. However, Bahrain did not renew the agreement when it ran out in June 1977. Under a new arrangement, MIDEASTFOR will no longer be homeported in Bahrain, but will be allowed to call there, and some MIDEASTFOR personnel will be allowed to remain on shore.

Despite the political changes in the gulf since 1973, U.S. political and strategic policies have remained basically the same: dependence on regional cooperation and a limited U.S. military presence.[12] Ironically, by 1975, considerable congressional opposition had developed to the "two pillar" policy on the grounds that it was creating an arms race in the gulf, particularly between Iran and Saudi Arabia. These two countries had indeed greatly accelerated arms purchases since 1973, but this was in large measure attributable to increased oil revenues rather than U.S. policy. The real question was what, if anything, should U.S. policy makers do about the situation.

The fourth principle of U.S. policy in the gulf addressed the Soviet threat and appeared to be more of an expression of hope than a principle of policy. The growing superpower detente implicit in the principle was based on mutual U.S.-Soviet interests in a global context that did not necessarily include the gulf.

Only the last principle addressed oil and economic interests, reflecting U.S. preoccupation with gulf security and relative complacency with the gulf oil situation on the very eve of the energy crisis. Mr. Sisco conceded that "we are witnessing rather dramatic changes in the terms of financial and concession arrangements between international oil companies and the producer states." But he went on to assert: "States such as Iran, Saudi Arabia and Kuwait, however, have consistently indicated by their approach to petroleum questions, their recognition of a strong mutual economic interest with the major industrial nations . . . [and] the useful role which the international companies play."[13]

Mr. Sisco was not the only one who failed to distinguish between strong political interests among these three countries in maintaining close ties with the United States and equally strong economic interests dictating oil policies not to the liking of either the United States or the oil companies. Despite the warnings of experts such as Ambassador James Akins,[14] few Americans were prepared for what was to come. The following year, the United States and the industrialized world witnessed an energy crisis from which the oil producers emerged in uncontested control of pricing and production of oil. The 1973 price rises and Arab oil embargo underscored the strategic importance of Persian Gulf oil. Since then, much of the attention of U.S. policy toward the gulf has been focused on the price and availability of oil and related economic matters.

In pursuit of overall economic goals, the United States sought to strengthen bilateral ties as well. On June 8, 1974, the United States and Saudi Arabia signed an agreement to expand cooperation in the fields of economics, technology, industry, and defense.[15] Joint commissions were subsequently established in each of the four fields. It was not intended to be a bilateral oil agreement, which would have been incompatible with the U.S. policy of seeking international cooperation both among the consumers and between them and the producers. But it was motivated by the recognition in the United States of the need for more bilateral cooperation.

The United States also signed an agreement with Iran in March 1975 to increase cooperation in various fields of economic development in Iran, including nuclear energy.[16]

A Look into the Future

Political and Strategic Interests

Given the political and strategic goals of U.S. Persian Gulf policy—
to foster political and internal stability so that the price and
availability of oil will not be precipitously altered for political
or military reasons—the policy was well conceived and implemented.[17] None of the gulf littoral states has succumbed to
radicalism. The long-dreaded but unexpected removal of King
Faysal from the throne of Saudi Arabia was followed by a smooth
transition in the succession of his half-brother, King Khalid. Many
of the destabilizing territorial disputes have been settled or at least
allowed to remain dormant. Iraq and Iran have achieved a measure
of rapprochement, ending the Kurdish insurgency; and in Oman,
the government seems to have the upper hand in the Dhufar insurgency. Soviet influence is no greater in the gulf than it was
before the British departed. And the Chinese presence is somewhat
smaller since their departure from Dhufar.

This rather rosy picture, however, fails to take into account that
U.S. Persian Gulf policy was designed to maintain a "low profile,"
and therefore its influence on regional stability has been at best
passive. One could argue that the security situation would have
turned out much the same no matter what the United States did,
but this is not precisely true. The fact that the United States did
not become directly involved in gulf security is probably one of
the most stabilizing courses it could have taken. Left to themselves, the gulf states have fared rather well, and there seems no
reason why the basic approach of moderate political support and
indirect security assistance should be changed.

It will be no longer possible, however, to maintain a low-profile
policy in the gulf. Many fears have been raised in the Congress and
elsewhere that military arms sales to the gulf will involve the
United States in gulf politics in a manner that could lead to
another Vietnam type of situation. Even if there were no arms
sales to the gulf, perhaps a quarter-million Americans are expected
to be residing in the gulf in the next decade, participating
in the development projects that are or will be launched
there. The human, political and economic implications of this
fact alone are enough to involve the United States deeply
in gulf affairs. There is a pressing need, therefore, to study the
impact that a large, private American community in the gulf

could have on policy options. To date, I know of no such studies being made.

In reviewing the "two pillar" policy, great as the inherent problems for Iranian-Arab, and particularly Iranian-Saudi, cooperation are, U.S. encouragement of such cooperation still provides the best security for U.S. interests, provided expectations are reasonably modest. Iran and Saudi Arabia are the two most important conservative states in the area, and by working together, they could go far to maintaining regional stability.

Evaluating the U.S. arms sales policy to the gulf is a bit more complicated. The implication of the critics is that the massive expansion of arms transfers to the area is highly destabilizing. This is diametrically counter to the rationale of the proponents, who say that arms sales to the gulf are intended to enhance regional security and stability by giving U.S. friends the means to defend themselves. In the opinion of this writer, there has never been any convincing empirical evidence to indicate that military inventories in and of themselves are either stabilizing or destabilizing. To measure stability, one must gauge the political climate as well as the intentions of the various leaders involved. If under certain circumstances a leader might harbor hostile intentions, then and only then does one look at his military capabilities and evaluate his military options, the constraints on these options, and the possible military repercussions of hostile acts he may initiate.

In the gulf area, the most likely antagonists in a conventional war are still Iraq and Iran, despite their current rapprochement. Both sides have concluded arms agreements greatly upgrading their inventories. The problem with evaluating arms sales agreements, however, is that they represent only a commitment. The actual deliveries are generally spaced out over a considerable period of time. Even accounting for this, it is hard to estimate the capacity of the purchasers to effectively absorb the equipment. Any attempt at an estimate must take into account such factors as training, manpower resources, and experience.

In the case of Iraq and Iran, while Iran may have the edge in the quality and quantity of equipment and in training programs for many weapons system categories, no Iranians except the two battalions that have seen duty in Oman have ever had any combat experience. The Iraqi armed forces, on the other hand, despite the political and other inherent weaknesses in their armed forces (e.g., good professional officers are distrusted and retired early in many cases as threats to the regime), have had combat and strategic logistical experience, most recently in the October 1973 war. In sum, despite new military acquisitions on both sides, it would be very difficult to assess the capabilities of Iraq and Iran in a war. Most observers go only so far as to say that both could probably defend their own territory but neither could probably mount a successful offensive against the other. Thus, it is not likely that the quantum increase in U.S. arms sales to Iran has had a major stabilizing or destabilizing effect in the context of a possible Iraqi-Iranian war.

Curiously enough, it is not a war between Iraq and Iran on which so much public attention has been focused in the context of U.S. arms transfers to the gulf, but a so-called arms race between Iran and Saudi Arabia, both recipients of U.S. arms. The most commonly imagined scenario of a confrontation between the two has Iran, arrogant and jingoistic with its huge armed forces, acting unilaterally on the Arab side of the gulf, perhaps to quell a radical uprising, but in a manner forcing Saudi Arabia to react with force. The danger of Iran miscalculating the Arab reaction to a unilateral Iranian military operation in the gulf is certainly serious—hence the U.S. policy to foster cooperation. But the shah sees the need to cooperate as well as anyone in the area. More importantly, in the context of arms sales, Iran had an overwhelming military superiority over all the conservative Arab states of the gulf, including Saudi Arabia, long before the current arms buildup and will continue to have one in the future. The present arms sales will do nothing materially to change that balance, even with a greater Saudi military capability. As to a possible Saudi-Iranian confrontation, both countries, despite their differences, see themselves as allies, not enemies. As mentioned above, the Saudis want a credible force in the gulf, not to fight Iran, but to have an independent voice in gulf security. In sum, the propensity of the Saudis and Iranians to cooperate is less influenced by U. S. arms sales than by a host of other factors.

The main threat to the security of the smaller gulf states is from internal subversion, not conventional military attack. Supersonic aircraft are scarcely appropriate to counter the threat of covert subversive activities; and in countering a coup attempt, a P-51 would probably be as effective as an F-14. Some of the smaller UAE shaykhdoms are so small that an F-14 would have trouble just staying within their borders at cruising speeds.

There are a number of U.S. domestic considerations relating to U.S. arms sales to the gulf which are as important as the effect of the sales on the area. One is the public image of the recipients. The shah has recently lost much of the popularity he once enjoyed in the U.S. Congress and among the general public. Long regarded as a key anticommunist ally and long-time friend, his popularity was strengthened by his cordial relations with Israel. Iran's lead in raising oil prices, however, cut into this popularity, and its more recent rapprochement with the Arab world including radical Iraq also has caused the shah's image in the United States to suffer. This loss of popularity, coming as it does in a period of general frustration over the Vietnam defeat and of determination by the U.S. Congress to play a more active role in foreign policy, even at the cost of reducing the flexibility crucial to diplomacy, has caused arms sales to Iran to be scrutinized more critically than ever before in the United States.

U.S. domestic reactions to arms sales to Saudi Arabia have always been ambivalent: positive because of Saudi Arabia's strident anti-communism, and negative because of its enmity to Israel and more recently its leadership in the Arab oil embargo. Despite the ambivalence, Saudi Arabia is undoubtedly viewed, because of its commanding oil reserves, as much more important to U.S. interests than it was just a few years ago. The domestic political shift can be seen in the irony of Vice-President Rockefeller, who boycotted King Faysal's visit to New York in 1965, representing the United States in Riyadh to extend condolences over the King's death ten years later.

U.S. domestic attitudes toward sales to Kuwait are also ambivalent, but probably less negative. This is because the principal threat to Kuwait's security comes from radical Iraq, and because its military role in any Arab-Israeli conflict would be symbolic at most. Also, the magnitude of U.S. arms sales to Kuwait is very small compared to sales to Iran and Saudi Arabia. Sales to other gulf states are even smaller.

U.S. domestic economic factors also play a role in attitudes toward arms sales to the gulf. The oil price rise was felt personally by all Americans, and further association of the price rise with the Arab embargo has produced a very negative reaction among many segments of the Congress and the public. This negative feeling was reinforced by the 1974-1975 recession, which many also blame on high oil prices. At the same time, the recession could be a powerful inducement to encourage arms sales. It may be difficult for the general public to see expanded arms sales in terms of advantages to the balance of payments, but in congressional districts with large defense industries and rising unemployment, the additional jobs created by export arms production became very convincing arguments for more sales.

In the face of all of these conflicting domestic and foreign factors, it is difficult to make specific recommendations for future arms sales policy in the gulf. Except for new sales agreements with the lower gulf states now qualifying for the first time as purchasers of arms, that policy has remained virtually unchanged for years. The principal restraint on the magnitude of the arms transfers was the ability of the gulf states to pay. Since 1973 that restraint has been removed. Should the United States react by imposing a political restraint to compensate for the removal of the economic restraint? (For example, an arms request could be refused on the grounds that more arms would be destabilizing.) This idea has a degree of support in the Congress, where there has been talk of legislation to further limit the size of arms sales transactions not requiring congressional approval (the current maximum is $25 million). Such a limitation could possibly reduce arms sales, but there is no guarantee that the gulf states would not go to Western Europe, or even the Soviet Union, if turned down by the United States. Moreover, it is not unlikely that any refusal based on political reasons, either by legislation or executive policy, would have an adverse effect on general U.S. relations with the requesting state.

It would seem to this writer that such an approach is far too simplistic. For one thing, there are already signs that some of the gulf states, despite increased oil revenues, are developing liquidity problems which will reimpose economic constraints on their ability to purchase arms. Moreover, arms requests from the others, chiefly Iran and Saudi Arabia, are too varied and complex to be treated in the aggregate.

It is quite likely, for example, that requests for more conventional types of weapons will taper off, at least for the next several years, as the gulf states' armed forces take delivery and attempt to absorb what is already on order. The integration of these new weapons systems will probably be impeded by the severe skilled-manpower shortages which have caused the public and private sectors of these countries to compete for good people.

On the other hand, Iran is already seeking to purchase F-14s to upgrade its airforce, and Saudi Arabia is looking for a follow-on aircraft for its aging Lightnings, which will become obsolescent by about 1978. The juxtaposition of aircraft purchases by these two countries will almost certainly renew public debate about a gulf arms race, although no deliveries would be made for several years, even assuming letters of offer were imminent.

In addition to aircraft, there will probably be a continuing interest, particularly by Iran, in purchasing the latest sophisticated weapons systems. The psychological appeal of such weapons is probably the greatest factor in such interest. In many cases, the United States is the only supplier, and much pressure can be applied by the prospective purchaser. Such pressure presents problems for the United States, not only politically, but also in terms of its own security requirements. One way of reacting to such requests, however, rather than refusing them out of hand, is to agree to consider sales, but only after U.S. needs and those of other allies already possessing signed letters of offers are met. In many cases, this would delay sales for a number of years, thus greatly retarding the buildup of such weapons systems in the area, without incurring unfavorable political reactions. Just meeting U.S. needs has already become a major problem in the post-Vietnam period.

In sum, each request and category of requests should be viewed on its own merits, taking into consideration the political, strategic, and economic impact of the arms transfer not only on the gulf region, but on the United States as well.

Finally, there is the question of MIDEASTFOR. Although Bahrain is no longer a homeport, and ships assigned to MIDEASTFOR will spend more time calling at other friendly ports, the new arrangement with Bahrain enables MIDEASTFOR to operate in the area without seeking new facilities. It would seem advantageous, therefore, for the United States to operate under the present circumstances so long as the arrangement is agreeable to all concerned.

In broader perspective, MIDEASTFOR is not primarily for a gulf interest but for a broader Indian Ocean interest, and as such is beyond the scope of this book. Its future basically centers around two questions: 1) Does the United States in fact need a permanently stationed naval force in the Indian Ocean, or can naval ships be rotated there on a regular basis? The latter option might become more attractive with the Suez Canal reopened, but would still necessitate a judgment of the overall benefit to the

United States of greater economic costs and lesser political costs in the region. 2) If a permanent Indian Ocean force is needed, does there also need to be a permanent shore installation? At present, the answer appears to be no. Should the present situation change, however, the only other politically practicable alternative site in the whole Indian Ocean at the moment is Diego Garcia, which is so far to the south that its economic and strategic suitability are somewhat questionable. Whatever the determination of U.S. strategic needs in the Indian Ocean, trying to maintain an installation without adequate regard for the political costs would clearly be a dubious undertaking.

Economic Interests

U.S. economic interests in the gulf fall into three broad categories: oil, monetary concerns, and commerce. In each case, the policies dealing with these interests far transcend the gulf.

Energy policy. There is a strong domestic concensus that the United States should be as independent from foreign sources of energy as possible. Project Independence, inaugurated in the aftermath of the 1973-1974 energy crisis and purported to be a "framework for developing a national energy policy,"[18] concentrated on how to accomplish less dependence on foreign supplies of oil. Nevertheless, at least through the medium term, the United States will be increasingly dependent on foreign, particularly Persian Gulf, oil. The reason is simple. U.S. supplies are being depleted, and the gulf has two-thirds of the free world's proved reserves. Thus, whatever energy goals the United States ultimately chooses, this fact must be accepted.

U.S. energy policy options toward the gulf producers must be analyzed in the context of OPEC so long as the OPEC members remain determined to act in concert on setting prices and production rates. As discussed in chapter 5, uncertainty about future supply-demand relationships makes the projection of the future state of energy-related matters extremely difficult. Identification of a few operating assumptions, however, might give some indication of the policy options available to deal with the foreign-supply side of the energy problem.

The first assumption is that OPEC is a rather narrowly conceived oil cartel, not a monolithic economic or political bloc. This assumption would argue for not treating OPEC as a political alliance, lest out of self-defense it begin to act like one. Algeria's President Boumedienne, who has long wished to politicize OPEC, scored a diplomatic coup when he announced at the March 1975 OPEC meeting that Iraq and Iran would agree to a rapprochement. This "political solidarity" was repeated at the April 7, 1975, preliminary OPEC conference, when the OPEC producers refused to back down from the Algerian position that a consumer-producer conference should include more on its agenda than oil prices. These developments have led some to conclude that OPEC is developing a new political dimension. But this type of solidarity costs the OPEC members nothing economically and enables them to gain politically in support from the third world. The real measure of political solidarity comes in collective measures where both political and economic costs are involved. Except on the subject of OPEC solidarity over oil prices, there are simply insufficient mutual political interests among the members to support broader political action beyond vocal support. Thus, despite the rhetoric, Algeria was not able to expand OPEC's scope to include a broader political dimension. On the other hand, U.S. and other policies could succeed where Boumedienne could not. Consumer countries that polarize all relations with the producers into a consumer-producer confrontation, and that state publicly that their aim is to crush OPEC, are merely inviting OPEC members to unite politically to withstand the consumer threat. It makes much more sense to develop a policy aimed at increasing mutual trust among the consumers and producers so that mutual recriminations do not poison the atmosphere surrounding negotiations on the real issues with which OPEC members and the consumers must deal: the future price of oil, and coping with the political, economic, and monetary problems arising out of the present price of oil. Thus, if OPEC members wish to have a broader dialogue on issues of world economy, third world development, and the like, why not? The producers know as well as the consumers that such talks will not change the price of oil, but they could certainly improve the atmosphere within which oil price negotiations will take place.

The second assumption is that OPEC members are determined to coordinate their policies. It would be foolish for the United States either to expect OPEC's imminent demise or to encourage it. A protracted consumer-producer confrontation would be an economic and political disaster for all concerned. One prominent U.S. official expressed the opinion that the United States could indeed force the price of oil down to two dollars a barrel. All that need be done is to create a world depression! In other words, the problem is not how to get the price of oil down, but at what cost—politically as well as economically. Whereas the consumers could indeed force the producers to their knees, it would most probably be at a price that any rational man should consider too high.

Since Dr. Kissinger's interview in the January 13, 1975, issue of *Business Week*, the option of military force in the Persian Gulf has been seriously studied as one means of bringing the producers to terms. The unfortunate element in Dr. Kissinger's statement was that many on both sides began to consider an essentially draconian response as possible in less than draconian circumstances. The substance of his statement was innocuous. It was essentially a tautology: that force would be used in circumstances (i.e., "strangulation") where no other alternative but force was left.

The secretary was apparently trying to communicate in tone rather than substance the urgency of coming to grips with the energy problem. Too many Western politicians have blamed the world's economic ills solely on the high price of oil; and too many OPEC member-nation politicians, recognizing that world inflation long predated high prices, have totally absolved themselves of any responsibilities for the world's economic problems. A sense of urgency and assumption of more responsibility is needed on both sides, but talk of using military force serves only to increase the sense of confrontation, not further cooperation.

Many Westerners, particularly those fearful that the Arab oil weapon will force the United States to abandon Israel, and those concerned that the high price of oil and shift of economic power to OPEC will undermine U.S. strategic power, have seen in the military option a simple way of solving the problems of the OPEC hold on oil prices and the Arab political power derived from oil. What the proponents of developing a military option have failed to take into account is the political, economic, moral, and human cost, not of taking the oil fields, but of holding them for as long as necessary, perhaps a century or more.

The producers, many of whom in recent memory have been under foreign rule, react to the threat of war very emotionally, even if they do not take the threat very seriously. Talk of war raises fears of Western, and particularly U.S., intentions. In such an atmosphere, it would be entirely possible for the Persian Gulf producers to adopt policies against their own economic and political interest merely in response to a perceived threat. In sum, no one can win a confrontation.

Yet another assumption is that actual cooperation is a long way from simply seeking to cooperate. Throughout a series of interviews with government and business officials both of major consuming countries and gulf producing countries, the writer was struck by the unanimity of views that consumer-producer cooperation was vital, but the absolute lack of consensus about what constituted cooperation. For some it seemed to embody the idea that if enough communication could be encouraged the problem would work itself out. Communication is undoubtedly vital, and it is true that to date there has been very little of it. But it is not enough. Cooperation must accommodate several basic and in some cases inconsistent demands:

The consumers want as low a price for oil as possible, and the producers as high a price. No amount of communication will obliterate that. Some accommodation must therefore be reached on the best way to meet both interests.

Secondly, the OPEC countries have certain political constraints against cooperation. They find it currently impossible to lower the money price of oil, particularly if it were to appear that they were reacting to any kind of pressure from the consumers. In addition, they are all committed to working collectively through OPEC on oil prices, and any attempt to split them on that issue would most certainly be resisted.

Recognizing these constraints, it does appear possible that accommodations can be made on all sides for the common good. The disturbing element of it all is that if the energy and world economic problems are not solved, the causes will probably be due to political factors—distrust, chauvinism, disproportionate influence of special interests, and short-sightedness—rather than to economic ones.

Monetary concerns. Since the four-fold oil price increases of 1973, there has been concern over the accumulation of monetary reserve holdings by a few oil-producing countries, particularly in the gulf. The magnitude of the problem has not reached the draconian proportions that were originally feared, but it is still serious. For example, Saudi Arabia's reserves surpassed those of the United

States in February 1975 to become second only to West Germany's.[19] By the end of 1977, Saudi Arabia is expected to have over $50 billion in foreign exchange reserves.

Since World War II, when current international monetary institutions were created, the United States and Western Europe have monopolized the monetary system. When Japan became an economic power it also joined what amounted to a very exclusive club. This group has been wrestling with the problem of petrodollar reserves since the issue reached major proportions after 1973. Now the oil producers are demanding an active role, commensurate with their new economic power, in developing whatever arrangements are eventually adopted to deal with the problem. In other words, the oil producers want to join the club. This has been a difficult demand for the industrialized world to accept, but in the end, it appears to be inevitable and the sooner accepted the better.

One option for encouraging the recycling of petrodollars is to encourage more investment by the gulf oil producers in the United States, the largest capital market in the free world. There are, however, significant psychological barriers to such investment. For the producers, there is the fear that their natural wealth, by being converted into long-term foreign investments, will shrink due to inflation and currency devaluations. "Recycling," stated Abd al-Latif al Hamad, director-general of the Kuwait Fund for Arab Economic Development, "is a good word, only if it should not be interpreted as just syphoning back petrofunds to rich oil importers in return for doubtful financial assets."[20]

In addition to fears that the industrial world will not put its economic house in order, the gulf producers fear that some Western states, including the United States, might hold their investments hostage for political reasons. In case of another Arab-Israeli war and subsequent Arab oil embargo, for example, the gulf Arab producers fear that the United States might freeze or even seize their assets in retaliation. Proof of hostile U.S. reception to Arab investments was seen by many gulf financiers in the highly publicized U.S. public opposition to private Saudi investors seeking to purchase controlling interest in banks in California and Detroit and to the Kuwaiti purchase of an island off South Carolina in 1974-1975.

Gulf fears of investing in the United States are matched by the fears of many in the United States that the gulf oil producers seek to "buy out" the country, or in the case of the Arabs at least, to use their financial power against Jewish financial interests. In 1974, N.M. Rothschild and Sons were not invited to bid on a $40 million Eurodollar bond issue because of Arab investors' objections; and early in 1975, the Kuwait International Investment Company withdrew from a group managing two Eurobond issues because of Jewish banking participation. In addition to the Rothschild banking interests, Lazard Frères and S.G. Warburg have also been boycotted.[21] The Arabs maintain that such banks are boycotted not because they are Jewish but because of support for Israel. Such activities, nevertheless, help to increase emotions against Arab and even non-Arab foreign investment in the United States. By March 1975 nearly forty bills had been introduced in the Congress ostensibly to monitor foreign investment but in many cases designed to halt investment in the United States by Arabs and other oil producers.

The U.S. banking community has recognized the folly of limiting foreign investment and has opposed it. In fact, much of the subsequent attention given to combatting the Arab boycott, according to a prominent Jewish financial expert, was to draw efforts away from attempts to limit foreign investment.

Since the summer of 1975 there have been signs of lessening mistrust, at least on the part of the gulf investors. Previously, their investment priorities were safety, liquidity, and return on investment, in that order. Recent investments have been more diversified and over a longer term than previously. Nevertheless, the seeds of mistrust are still there, and it would behoove the U.S. government to encourage and strengthen mutual trust to the extent possible. Foreign investment will not only accelerate domestic capital formation, but it will also give the investors a greater stake in the well-being of the U.S. economy.

Commerce. U.S. commercial opportunities in the gulf are large and growing larger. The combined planned expenditure for development projects in the area over the next five years, for example, is in the neighborhood of $250 billion. In five years, annual imports by gulf states could exceed $50 billion in current dollars, making the region one of the world's major trading areas, quite apart from oil sales.

A significant proportion of U.S. exports during this period will undoubtedly be on a government-to-government basis. The Foreign Military Sales program is a prime example. But tremendous opportunities will still exist for the private sector. Sales of goods and services fall into four categories: exports of consumer goods directly to gulf merchants; equity investments; management contracts; and "turnkey projects" opened to competitive public tender.

In the area of consumer exports, U.S. firms have a growing advantage with their generally higher-quality but also higher-priced goods. As the gulf consumer accumulates more income, his preferences for quality consumer goods is increasing. For example, in Saudi Arabia during the *hajj*, there are two distinct qualities of goods in many shops—cheap Chinese and other products for the *hajjis*, and more expensive U.S. and European goods for the Saudis.

Management contracts are available somewhat on a competitive basis, but often go to firms having long-standing relationships with the countries in question. The oil companies, for example, will ultimately be offered management contracts to operate the production facilities they developed. In Saudi Arabia, TWA has a management contract with Saudi Arabian Airlines, which it helped to create.

In the field of equity investment, the gulf states, in both the public and private sectors, are not so much interested in capital inputs as they are in a firm's special technology, markets, or some other asset that can be utilized. For example, Iran's investment in Krupp's steel production was made with Iran's budding steel industry in mind. Moreover, equity holdings tend to induce the foreign participant to be concerned for the long-run success of the venture.

It is in turnkey projects where the largest expenditure will probably be made. Typically, gulf leaders, anxious to provide for the economic and social development of their peoples, are attempting to create instant progress; and because of their huge financial assets, they are willing to absorb a very high cost for it. The current Saudi five-year plan alone calls for an expenditure of $142 billion for a population of less than 4 million Saudis and perhaps 1 million resident aliens.

The United States has a general policy of export promotion throughout the world. The Department of Commerce has created an Office of Export Development for this purpose. Overseas, embassies are staffed with commercial officers to aid U.S.

businessmen abroad and to report commercial information to Washington, where it is made available to the public. The Commerce Department also organizes trade fairs and other trade-promotion activities. The U.S. Export-Import Bank also has a major export-promotion function in helping to finance U.S. export portions of development projects abroad.

The creation of four new embassies in the gulf in 1972—in Bahrain, Qatar, the UAE, and Oman—was justified largely in terms of U.S. commercial interests. Nevertheless, the embassies originally were woefully underfinanced, each with a nonresident ambassador in the person of the U.S. ambassador to Kuwait. As it turned out, the American Embassy in Kuwait was incapable, from both a personnel and a funding standpoint, of adequately providing administrative and other support to the new embassies. The small embassy staffs became completely inundated after the oil price rises, as thousands of U.S. businessmen trekked to the gulf to try to tap the new oil wealth. Finally, in 1974, the new posts were enlarged with the addition of resident ambassadors. Their main function remains trade promotion.

The U.S. private sector has a great comparative advantage in the universally high regard for American technology and quality. The larger U.S. firms also have the advantage of huge assets from which they can draw in bidding for contracts. There are, however, some special disadvantages in the way business is conducted in the gulf and the Middle East generally.

The most visible disadvantage is in having to pay middlemen or "agents" huge sums in order to obtain business. In the gulf a payment for a service rendered is acceptable, whereas in the United States it may be considered a bribe. If there is U.S. government participation in the project, moreover, the U.S. firm could possibly find itself liable for criminal prosecution.

A second disadvantage is more or less self-inflicted in the form of legislative opposition to the Arab boycott of Israel. Although the boycott has been in existence for almost thirty years, it was not until 1975, in the wake of the Arab oil embargo and OPEC oil price rises, that the boycott became a political issue in the United States. In 1975, a congressional subcommittee began to investigate compliance with the boycott by U.S. firms, and the Federal Reserve System issued new orders limiting bank compliance in boycott requests. Despite measures by the executive branch to persuade the Arabs to limit some of the more objectionable (from the U.S. point of view) practices of the boycott, various members of Congress tried in 1976 to obtain more sweeping legislative restrictions. Their efforts failed, but the boycott became a minor presidential campaign issue that year and a new attempt was made in 1977. In June 1977, President Carter signed into law an extension of the Export Administration Act, which substantially prohibits U.S. firms from discriminating against other U.S. firms "blacklisted" by the Arab League Boycott Commission, and which also limits the degree to which firms can comply with requests for boycott information.

The new law does not attempt to oppose the sovereign right of the Arab states to regulate their commerce with other countries, and in many cases procedural changes can meet the new statute requirements. Nevertheless, given the firm convictions of several Arab states—particularly Saudi Arabia—regarding the boycott, it is possible that these provisions will have the effect of restricting the volume of U.S. business in the Arab states and consequently the level of U.S. esteem and influence.

The sheer magnitude of some projects is also a problem. Some of the larger turnkey projects will cost well over 1 billion dollars, and may extend over ten or twelve years. Commonly, gulf states call for a fixed-price contract and then require a bid bond of 2 or 3 percent of the project cost, a performance bond of up to 10 percent of the project, and an advance repayment guarantee equal to the funds advanced by the contracting country. It is the performance bond that has been a particular problem for American firms because of the magnitude of the projects and the size of the assets that must be pledged to obtain financing. Moreover, agent fees often can run the cost of a project up as much as an extra 35 percent.

For projects so large and stretched over such a long period of time, it is next to impossible to predict costs. Inflation, bottlenecks (particularly manpower shortages), and other unknowns make fixed-cost contracts extremely risky. In addition, the assets which a company must have to obtain financing for such projects are so great as to dissuade many U.S. firms from competing even if they are technologically competent to provide the best product at the cheapest price.

Conflict of interest and antitrust laws preclude the U.S. government from subsidizing American firms in their bids on such projects; but the same is not true for European or Japanese firms.

Their governments regularly subsidize them with low- or no-interest loans, loan guarantees, and protection against escalating costs. Although the Export-Import Bank does participate in some debt financing, there is no comparison between its activities and the activities of those governments.

To deal with these problems, there are a number of policy options the United States could take. One is to encourage a higher standard of business practices in the gulf than is now the rule. Even without eliminating agents, fees could be routinized according to regular schedules and hence become more accountable.

The United States could also try to persuade the gulf states to improve their bidding procedures. Fixed-cost contracts of such magnitude, for example, are not only risky but unnecessarily expensive since the bidder must err on the high side of projected cost escalations; a cost-plus-a-percentage-profit contract would not only be less expensive but also less risky to the bidder. Also, large projects could advantageously be broken down to component parts, to allow more flexibility. This would additionally make bids more competitive, as smaller firms would be able to bid, resulting in lower costs.

Finally, the United States could try to persuade European and Japanese governments not to subsidize the bids their companies make. Since that course is almost certain to fail, the United States might consider broadening the mandate of the Export-Import Bank to allow loans and guarantees competitive with public financing in other countries for firms not large enough to obtain sufficient financing in the private sector.

In sum, U.S. policy toward the gulf has adequately fulfilled U.S. political, strategic, and economic interests. There is no cause for complacency, however. The gulf is politically stable only when measured by Middle Eastern standards, which are tenuous indeed. Arms race or no, the large arms transfers to the area bear watching. And not only are future oil supply-demand relationships hard to project, but equally difficult will be projecting the social, economic, and political change brought about by petrodollar development expenditures. It is vital that Americans become aware of these issues, for with two-thirds of the free world's proved oil reserves, the gulf will remain of major importance to the United States for a long time to come.

NOTES

[1]Herman Frederick Eilts, "Ahamd Bin Na'aman's Mission to the United States in 1840: The Voyage of the Al-Sultana to New York City" (Muscat, Oman: Petroleum Development (Oman), n.d); reprinted from the Essex Institute *Quarterly*, October 1962, p. 72.

[2]Thomas Bailey, *A Diplomatic History of the American People*, 6th ed. (New York: Appleton-Century-Crofts, 1958), p. 301.

[3]William D. Brewer, "United States Interests in the Persian Gulf" (paper delivered at the Princeton University Conference on Middle East Focus: The Persian Gulf, October 24, 25, 1968), p.3.

[4]B.C. Busch, *Britain and the Persian Gulf, 1894-1914* (Berkeley: University of California Press, 1967), p. 25.

[5]For an account of the early history of the Arabian Mission, see Alfred DeWitt Mason and Frederick J. Barney, *History of the Arabian Mission* (New York: Board of Foreign Missions of the Reformed Church in America, 1926). For a later period, see Dorothy Van. Ess, *History of the Arabian Mission, 1926-1957* (unpublished manuscript, archives of the Reformed Church in America), and Van Ess, *Pioneers in the Arab World* (Grand Rapids, Mich.: Eerdmans, 1975).

[6]Van Ess, *Pioneers in the Arab World*, pp. 104-108.

[7]Arabian Mission, Muscat, M.S., Ltr., Jalalat al Sultan Qaboos bin Said, Sultan of Oman to The Chief Administrator, American Mission, Muscat, August 15, 1970.

[8]Donald Bosch and John Buteyn, "Reflections on Two Years Cooperation With the Oman Ministry of Health" (Muscat, unpublished pamphlet, 1972).

[9]Oman, Ministry of Health, "Letter of agreement from Said S. Shakay, Director of Administration, to the General Programme Council of the Reformed Church in America, 21 December, 1970".

[10]*Washington Evening Star*, January 17, 1968.

[11]United States, Department of State, *Bulletin* (Washington, D.C.: Government Printing Office), vol. 67, no. 1732, p. 242.

[12]See, for example, "Opening Statement of Joseph J. Sisco, Undersecretary of State for Political Affairs Before the Special Subcommittee on Investigations, House International Relations Committee, June 10, 1975."

13*Ibid.*, p. 244.

14See James E. Akins, "The Oil Crisis: This Time the Wolf is Here," *Foreign Affairs* 51 (April 1973): 462-90.

15For the text of the agreement, see "Joint Statement on U.S.-Saudi Cooperation," Washington, D.C., June 8, 1974, Department of State, *News Release,* June 10, 1974.

16See "U.S.-Iran Joint Commission, Joint Communique, March 4, 1975," *Middle East Journal* 29 (Summer 1975): 345.

17Parts of this section were developed and expanded from an earlier paper by the writer, "U.S. Strategic Interests in the Persian Gulf: Problems and Policy Analysis," delivered at the National Security Affairs Conference of the National War College, Washington, D.C., July 14-15, 1975.

18See United States, Federal Energy Administration, *Project Independence* (Washington, D.C.: Government Printing Office, Nov. 1974).

19International Monetary Fund, *International Financial Statistics,* vol. 28, no. 8 (August 1975), p. 321.

20Abdlatif Y. Al-Hamad, "International Finance—An Arab Point of View" (speech delivered at the Algonquin Club, Boston, Mass., September 26, 1974).

21*The Economist,* vol. 254, no. 6860 (Feb. 1975), p. 82.

Appendix

Note: An attempt has been made to keep statistical data presented in the text at a minimum for two reasons. Not only is the accuracy of data from this part of the world highly uneven, but with the phenomenal pace of change in the gulf, most data tend to be out of date even by the time they become available. The following tables therefore represent only a few basic figures designed to aid the reader.

TABLE 1
THE PERSIAN GULF STATES
BASIC DATA

States	Ruler (and date of accession)	Capital	Area (sq. mi.)	Approx. Population (thousands)	Armed Forces		
					Army	Air Force	Navy
Major States							
Iran	Muhammad Reza Shah Pahlevi (Sept. 1941)	Tehran	636,000	33,000	165,000	57,000	13,000
Iraq	General Ahmad Hassan al-Bakr (July 1968)	Baghdad	172,000	11,000	90,000	10,000	2,000
Saudi Arabia	King Khalid bin Abd al-Aziz Al Saud (Mar. 1975)	Riyadh	830,000[1]	4,000	33,000[2]	6,000	1,000
Smaller States							
Kuwait	Amir Sabah al-Salim Al Sabah (Nov. 1965)	Kuwait	7,800[3]	1,000	6,000	2,000	200
Bahrain	Shaykh Isa bin Salman al-Khalifah (Nov. 1961)	Manama	213	234	1,200	—	—
Qatar	Shaykh Khalifah bin Hamad Al Thani (Feb. 1972)	al-Dowha (Doha)	4,000	159	1,200	50	50
UAE	President:Shaykh Zayd bin Sultan Al Nuhayyan (Dec. 1971)	Abu Dhabi	36,000[1]	235	9,500	350	150
Abu Dhabi	Shaykh Zayd bin Sultan Al Nuhayyan (1966)	Abu Dhabi	32,000[1]	75	—	—	—

Smaller States
(cont'd.)

Dubai	Shaykh Rashid bin Said al-Maktm (1958)	Dubai	1,500	75	—	—	—
Sharjah	Shaykh Sultan bin Muhammad al-Qasimi (Jan. 1972)	Sharjah	1,000	35	—	—	—
Ajman	Shaykh Rashid bin Humayd al-Nu'aymi (al-Na'imi) (1928)	Ajman	100	5	—	—	—
Umm al-Qaywayn	Shaykh Ahmad bin Rashid al-Mu'alla (1929)	Umm al-Qaywayn	300	5	—	—	—
Ras al-Khaymah	Shaykh Saqr bin Muhammad al-Qasimi (1948)	Ras al-Khaymah	650	30	250	—	—
Fujayrah	Shaykh Hamad bin Muhammad al-Sharqi (1974)	Fujayrah	450	10	—	—	—
Oman	Sultan Qabus bin Said Al Bu Said (1970)	Muscat	82,000[1]	710	9,000[4]	400	200

[1]In the absence of totally delimited borders, this is only an approximation.

[2]There is in addition a National Guard of approximately equal strength.

[3]Including annexed areas of the Saudi-Kuwaiti Neutral Zone

[4]There were at the end of 1975 1,500 Iranians and about an equal number of Jordanians stationed in Oman.

Table 2
THE PERSIAN GULF STATES
BASIC ECONOMIC DATA

States	Oil Income 1975 (billions)	Imports 1975 (billions)	Unit of Currency	$ Exchange Rate per 1 Unit
Major States				
Iran	$18.7	$13.2	Iranian Rial	$ .014
Iraq	8.1	6.1	Iraqi Dinar	3.38
Saudi Arabia	27.3	6.5	Saudi Riyal	.28
Smaller States				
Kuwait	8.0	2.1	Kuwaiti Dinar	3.46
Bahrain	.5	.4	Bahrain Dinar	2.53
Qatar	1.9	.6	Qatar Riyal	.25
U.A.E.	6.7	2.6	U.A.E. Dirham	.25
Oman	1.8	—	Omani Rial	2.90

Source: Oil income for Oman is my estimate. All other figures for oil income and imports are from U.S. Treasury Department, July 1976.
Exchange Rates: As of February 1977; source: IMF, *International Financial Statistics*, April 1977.

Table 3
THE PERSIAN GULF STATES
BASIC OIL DATA

States	Proved Oil Reserves, end of 1976 (million bbl.)	Crude Production, 1976 (million bd.)	Capacity, Nov. 1976 (million bd.)
Major States			
Iran	63,000	5.9	6.6
Iraq	34,000[1]	2.1	3.0
Saudi Arabia	110,000	8.6	11.8
Smaller States			
Kuwait	67,400	1.8	3.3
Bahrain	290	.06	—
Qatar	5,707	.5	.7
U.A.E.			
Abu Dhabi	29,000	1.6	2.0
Dubai	1,500	.3	.3
Sharjai	1,700	.04	.05
Oman	5,800	.4	—

Source: Crude production figures from *The Oil and Gas Journal,* December 27, 1976, p. 29; reserve figures from *The Oil and Gas Journal,* December 29, 1975, p. 86; capacity figures from *Petroleum Intelligence Weekly,* Jan. 3, 1976, p. 7.
[1]Some experts believe Iraqi reserves are actually much greater than this.

...dons and Oman, the British military and political presence was still considered to be the major stabilizing force. On January 16, 1968, British Prime Minister Harold Wilson announced to the House of Commons

> We have decided to accelerate the withdrawal of our forces from their stations in the Far East... by the end of 1971... We have also decided to withdraw our forces from the Persian Gulf by the same date... On the Gulf, we have indicated to the Governments concerned that our basic interest in the prosperity of the area remains, and as I have said... the capability we shall be maintaining here will be available...

The announcement came as a surprise to many, both in the gulf and beyond it. After 150 years, the British were relinquishing their security role. And it was an abrupt ending. When the Conservative party came to power in Britain in June 1970, it considered reversing this decision—or at least postponing the 1971 deadline. It soon realized, however, that with Iranian and Arab opinion firmly op-

Selected Bibliography

The following selections are suggested for additional reading. For more comprehensive references, see the bibliographical sections of the American University's *Area Handbook for Iran* (Washington, D.C., 1971); *Area Handbook for Saudi Arabia* (1970); and *Area Handbook for the Peripheral States of the Arabian Peninsula* (1971). See also J.D. Anthony, *The States of the Arabian Peninsula and Gulf Littoral: A Selected and Partially Annotated Bibliography* (Washington, D.C.: The Middle East Institute, 1973), and C.L. Geddes, *Analytical Guide to the Bibliography on the Arabian Peninsula* (Denver, Colo.: American Institute of Islamic Studies, 1974).

DOCUMENTS

Great Britain. *Memorial of the Government of the United Kingdom of Great Britain and Northern Ireland in Arbitration Concerning Buraimi and the Common Frontier Between Abu Dhabi and Saudi Arabia.* 2 vols. London, 1955.

Iran, Ministry of Foreign Affairs. *Iran's Foreign Policy: A Compendium of the Writings and Statements of His Imperial Majesty Shahanshah Aryamehr.* Tehran, n.d.

Oman, Ministry of Development, National Statistical Department, *Development in Oman. 1970-1974.* Muscat, Oman, 1975.

Qatar, Ministry of Information. *Qatar in the Seventies.* Doha, Qatar, 1973.

Saudi Arabia. *Memorial of the Government of Saudi Arabia in the Arbitration for the Settlement of the Territorial Dispute between Muscat and Abu Dhabi on One Side and Saudi Arabia on the Other.* Cairo, 1955.

United Arab Emirates, Ministry of Foreign Affairs. *United Arab Emirates.* Prepared by the Centre for Documentation and Research. Abu Dhabi and London: Finsbury Printing Company, 1972.

United States, Congress, House of Representatives. *Means of Measuring Naval Power with Special Reference to U.S. and Soviet Activities in the Indian Ocean.* Prepared for the Subcommittee on the Near East and South Asia of the Committee on Foreign Affairs by the Foreign Affairs Division, Congressional Research Service, Library of Congress. Washington, D.C., May 12, 1974.

——————. *New Perspectives on the Persian Gulf.* Ninety-third Congress, 1st Session, June 6, July 17, 23, 24, and Nov. 28, 1973. Washington, D.C., 1973.

——————. *U.S. Interests In and Toward the Persian Gulf.* Hearings before the Subcommittee on the Near East of the Committee on Foreign Affairs, February 2, June 7, August 8, 15, 1972. Washington, D.C., 1972.

——————. *The Persian Gulf 1974: Money, Politics, Arms and Power.* Ninety-third Congress, 2nd Session, July 30, Aug. 5, 7, 12, 1974. Washington, D.C., 1975.

United States, Federal Trade Commission. *The International Al Cartel.* Published by the Select Committee on Small Business, U.S. Senate, 82nd Congress, 2nd Session. Washington, D.C., 1952.

United States, Department of Treasury, United States-Saudi Arabian Joint Commission on Economic Cooperation. *Summary of Saudi Arabian Five Year Development Plan (1975-1980).* Washington, D.C., 1975.

BOOKS AND MONOGRAPHS

Abir, Mordechai. *Oil, Power and Politics: Conflict in Arabia, The Red Sea and the Gulf.* London: Frank Cass, 1974.

Abu Hakima, Ahmad M. *A History of Eastern Arabia.* Beirut, Lebanon: Khayats, 1965.

Aitchison, C.U. *A Collection of Treaties, Engagements and Sanads Relating to India and Neighboring Countries.* Vol. 11. Calcutta, 1892.

Amin, Abdul Amir. *British Interests in the Persian Gulf, 1747-1778.* Leiden, Netherlands: Brill, 1967.

Anthony, John Duke. *The Arab States of the Lower Gulf: People, Politics, Petroleum.* Washington, D.C.: The Middle East Institute, 1975.

Bayne, E.A. *Persian Kingship in Transition.* New York: American Universities Field Staff, 1968.

Belgrave, James H.D. *Welcome to Bahrain.* 8th ed. Bahrain: Augustan Press, 1973.

Bill, James A. *The Politics of Iran: Groups, Classes and Modernization.* Columbus, Ohio: Charles E. Merrill, 1972.

Burrell, R.M. *The Persian Gulf* The Washington Papers, no. 1. Washington, D.C.: Center for Strategic and International Studies, 1972.

—————, and Cottrell, Alvin J. *Iran, The Arabian Peninsula and The Indian Ocean.* Strategy Papers, no. 14. New York: National Strategy Information Center, 1972.

Busch, Briton C. *Britain and the Persian Gulf, 1894-1914.* Berkeley: University of California Press, 1967.

Chubin, Shahram, and Zabih, Sepehr. *The Foreign Policy of Iran: A Developing State in a Zone of Great Power Conflict.* Berkeley: University of California Press, 1974.

Cole, Donald Powell. *Nomads of the Nomads: The Al Murrah Bedouin of the Empty Quarter.* Chicago: Aldine Publishing Co., 1975.

Coon, Carlton S. *Caravan: The Story of the Middle East.* Rev. ed. New York: Henry Holt and Company, 1958.

Cooper, Charles A., and Alexander, Sydney S., eds. *Economic Development and Population Growth in the Middle East.* New York: American Elsevier Publishing Company, 1972.

De Gaury, Gerald, *Faisal: King of Saudi Arabia.* London: Arthur Barker, 1966.

Fenelon, Kevin G. *The United Arab Emirates: An Economic and Social Survey.* London: Longman, 1973.

Fiennes, Ranulf. *Where Soldiers Fear to Tread.* London, Sydney, Auckland, Toronto: Hodder and Stoughton, 1975.

Freeman, S. David. *Energy: The New Era.* New York: Vintage Books, 1974.

Halliday, Fred. *Arabia without Sultans.* London: Penguin Books, 1974.

Hawley, Donald F. *The Trucial States.* New York: Humanities Press, 1971.

Hay, Sir Rupert. *The Persian Gulf States.* Washington, D.C.: The Middle East Institute, 1959.

Hewins, Ralph. *A Golden Dream: The Miracle of Kuwait.* London: W.H. Allen, 1963.

——————. *Mr. Five Percent: The Story of Calouste Gulbenkian.* New York: Rinehart and Company, 1958.

Holden, David. *Farewell to Arabia.* London: Faber and Faber, 1966.

Howarth, David. *The Desert King: Ibn Saud and His Arabia.* New York: McGraw-Hill, 1964.

Hurewitz, J.C. *Diplomacy in the Near and Middle East, A Documentary Record: 1535-1914.* 2 vols. Princeton, N.J.: D. Van Nostrand Company, 1956.

Katakura, Motoko. *Bedouin Village.* Tokyo: University of Tokyo Press, 1977.

Kelly, John B. *Britain and the Persian Gulf, 1795-1880.* London: Oxford University Press, 1967.

——————. *Eastern Arabian Frontiers.* New York: Praeger, 1964.

Khadduri, Majid. *Independent Iraq.* London: Oxford University Press, 1951.

——————, ed. *Major Middle Eastern Problems in International Law.* Washington, D.C.: American Enterprise Institute of Public Policy Research, 1972.

——————. *Republican Iraq: A Study in Iraqi Politics Since the Revolution of 1958.* London: Oxford University Press, 1969.

Knauerhase, Ramon. *The Saudi Arabian Economy.* New York: Praeger, 1975.

Lambton, A.K.S. *The Persian Land Reform, 1962-1966.* Oxford: Clarendon Press, 1969.

Landen, Robert G. *Oman Since 1856: Disruptive Modernization in a Traditional Arab Society.* Princeton, N.J.: Princeton University Press, 1967.

Lenczowsky, George, ed. *Political Elites in the Middle East.* Washington, D.C.: American Enterprise Institute of Public Policy Research, 1975.

Long, David E. *Confrontation and Cooperation in the Gulf.* Middle East Problem Paper no. 10. Washington, D.C.: The Middle East Institute, 1974.

Long, David E. *Saudi Arabia.* The Washington Papers, vol. 4, no. 39. Beverly Hills and London: Sage Publications, 1976.

Longrigg, Stephen Hensley. *Oil In the Middle East: Its Discovery and Development.* London: Oxford University Press, 1968.

Lorimer, J.G. *Gazetteer of the Persian Gulf, Oman and Central Arabia.* 2 vols. Calcutta: Superintendent of Government Printing, 1915.

El-Mallakh, Ragaei. *Economic Development and Regional Cooperation: Kuwait.* Chicago: University of Chicago Press, 1968.

Malone, Joseph J. *The Arab Lands of Western Asia.* Englewood Cliffs, N.J.: Prentice-Hall, 1973.

Marlowe, John. *The Persian Gulf in the Twentieth Century.* New York: Praeger, 1962.

Mason, Alfred DeWitt, and Barney, Frederick J. *History of the Arabian Mission.* New York: Board of Missions of the Reformed Church in America, 1926.

Mikdashi, Zuhayr M. *The Community of Oil Exporting Countries.* Ithaca, N.Y.: Cornell University Press, 1972.

Nakhleh, Emile A. *Arab-American Relations in the Persian Gulf.* Foreign Affairs Study no. 17. Washington, D.C.: American Enterprise Institute for Public Policy Research, 1975.

_____. *The United States and Saudi Arabia: A Policy Analysis.* Washington, D.C.: American Enterprise Institute for Public Policy Research, 1975.

Owen, Roderic. *The Golden Bubble: Arabian Gulf Documentary.* London: Collins, 1957.

Pachachi, Nadim. *The Role of OPEC in the Emergence of New Patterns in Government-Company Relations.* London: Royal Institute of International Affairs, 1972.

Pahlevi, H.I.M. Muhammad Reza Shah. *Mission For My Country.* New York: McGraw-Hill, 1961.

_____. *The White Revolution.* Tehran, 1967.

Philby, H. St. John B. *Arabia.* London: Ernest Benn, 1930.

——————. *Arabian Jubilee*. London: Robert Hale, 1952.

Price, D.L. *Oman: Insurgency and Development*. Conflict Studies, no. 53 London: The Institute for the Study of Conflict, January 1975.

Qubain, Fahim. *Education and Science in the Arab World*. Baltimore: Johns Hopkins Press, 1966.

Ramazani, Rouhallah K. *Iran's Foreign Policy 1941-1973*. Charlottesville: University of Virginia Press, 1975.

——————. *The Persian Gulf: Iran's Role*. Charlottesville: University of Virginia Press, 1972.

Sadik, Muhammad T., and Snavely, William P. *Bahrain, Qatar and the United Arab Emirates: Colonial Past, Present Problems and Future Prospects*. Lexington, Mass., Toronto, and London: Lexington Books, D.C. Heath Company, 1972.

Stephens, Robert. *The Arab's New Frontier*. London: Temple Smith, 1973.

Stocking, George W. *Middle East Oil: A Study in Political and Economic Controversy*. Nashville, Tenn.: Vanderbilt University Press, 1970.

Tahtinen, Dale R. *Arms in the Persian Gulf*. Washington, D.C.: American Enterprise Institute of Public Policy Research, 1974.

Thesiger, Wilfred. *The Marsh Arabs*. London: Longmans, 1964.

Townsend, John. *Oman: The Making of a Modern State*. London: Croom Helm, 1975.

Van Ess, Dorothy, *Pioneers in the Arab World*. Grand Rapids, Mich.: Eerdmans, 1975.

Wells, Donald A. *Saudi Arabian Development Strategy*. Washington, D.C.: American Enterprise Institute for Public Policy Research, 1976.

Wilson, Arnold T. *The Persian Gulf: An Historical Sketch from the Earliest Times to the Beginning of the Twentieth Century*. London, Allen and Unwin, 1959.

Winder, R. Boyly. *Saudi Arabia in the Nineteenth Century*. London: Macmillan; New York: St. Martins Press, 1965.

Yar-Shater, Ehsan, ed. *Iran Faces the Seventies*. Praeger Special Studies for International Economics and Development. New York: Praeger, 1971.

Zonis, Marvin. *The Political Elite of Iran*. Princeton, N.J.: Princeton University Press, 1971.

ARTICLES, PAPERS, AND SPECIAL REPORTS

Adelman, M.A. "Is the Oil Shortage Real? Oil Companies as OPEC Tax Collectors." *Foreign Policy,* no. 9 (Winter 1972-1973), pp. 69-107.

Akins, James E. "The Oil Crisis: This Time the Wolf is Here." *Foreign Affairs* 51 (April 1973): 462-90.

Amouzegar, Jahangir. "The Oil Story: Facts, Fiction and Fair Play." *Foreign Affairs* 51 (July 1973): 676-89.

Anthony, John D. "The Union of Arab Amirates." *Middle East Journal* 26 (1972): 271-87.

Bosch, Donald, and Buteyn, John. "Reflections on Two Years Cooperation with the Oman Ministry of Health." Unpublished pamphlet of the American Mission in Muscat.

Brewer, William. "Yesterday and Tomorrow in the Persian Gulf." *Middle East Journal* 23 (1969): 149-58.

Chase Manhattan Bank. *Capital Investment of the World Petroleum Industry.* New York, December 1974.

_____. *The Profit Situation: A Special Petroleum Report.* New York, April 1974.

Erb, Richard. "The Financial Management Problem From the Perspective of OPEC Members." Paper delivered to the Council on Foreign Relations, New York, July 11, 1975.

Fallah, Reza. "The Energy Crisis: Its Origins and Suggested Remedies." Address delivered before the Center International d'Etudes Monetaires et Bancaires, Geneva, November 28-30, 1974.

Hashimi, Rasoul M.H., and Edwards, Alfred L. "Land Reform in Iraq: Economic and Social Implications." *Land Economics*, vol. 37, 1 (Feb. 1961).

Khadduri, Majid. "Iran's Claim to the Sovereignty of Bahrain." *American Journal of International Law* 45 (1951): Supplements, pp. 631-47.

Lauterpacht, E. "River Boundaries: Legal Aspects of the Shatt al Arab

Frontier." *International and Comparative Law Quarterly* 9 (1960): 208-236.

Liebesny, Herbert J. "Administrative and Legal Development in Arabia: The Persian Gulf Principalities." *Middle East Journal* 10 (1956): 33-42.

Long, David E. "The Politics of OPEC." Paper delivered to the Council on Foreign Relations, New York, April 22, 1975.

—————. "U.S. Strategic Interests in the Persian Gulf: Problems and Policy Analysis." Paper delivered to the Second Annual National Security Affairs Conference, The National War College, Fort McNair, Washington, D.C., July 14-15, 1975.

—————. "United States Policy Toward the Persian Gulf." *Current History,* no. 402 (Feb. 1975), pp. 69-85.

McNamara, Robert. Annual address to the World Bank reprinted in the *Summary Proceedings of the 1974 Annual Meeting of the Board of Governors.*

Middle East Institute. *The Arabian Peninsula, Iran and the Gulf States: New Wealth, New Power.* A Summary Record of the 27th Annual Conference of the Middle East Institute. Washington, D.C., Sept. 28-29, 1973.

—————. *The United States and the Middle East: Changing Relationships.* Proceedings of the 29th Annual Conference of the Middle East Institute, Washington, D.C., Oct. 3-4, 1975.

—————. *World Energy Demands and the Middle East.* Proceedings of the 26th Annual Conference of the Middle East Institute, Washington, D.C., Sept. 29-30, 1972.

Searby, Daniel M. "Doing Business in the Mideast: The Game is Rigged." *Harvard Business Review* 54, (Jan.-Feb. 1976): 56-64.

Turck, Nancy. "The Arab Boycott of Israel," *Foreign Affairs* 55 (April 1977): 472-93.